INVITATION TO A JOURNEY

A Seven-week Journey
Of Listening, Learning,
Loving And Praising!

BY ROBERT J. STYCZYNSKI

Fairway Press
Lima, Ohio

INVITATION TO A JOURNEY

FIRST EDITION
Copyright © 1992 by
Robert J. Styczynski

All rights reserved. No portion of this book may be reproduced or utilized in any form or by any means, electronic or mechanical including photocopying, without permission in writing from the publisher. Inquiries should be addressed to: Fairway Press, 628 South Main Street, Lima, Ohio 45804.

7940 / ISBN 1-55673-490-5   PRINTED IN U.S.A.

This book is dedicated to the greater glory of God, the One who is my greatest love, for He has favored me with His presence and with a joyful daily communion. He has gifted me with the companionship of a lovely wife who is my best friend, and with five loving children and grandchildren. He has been kind enough to provide me with two people who have been, from the beginning, faithful believers in His word as presented in this book — my wife, Nancy, and a friend, Ethel McKegg.

Invitation To A Journey

I invite you to join with me in a seven week journey of listening, learning, loving and praising through daily communion with God. It is the journey of a lifetime — your lifetime.

Robert

Contents

Preface		9
A Daily Prayer		11

WEEK 1

Monday	The Journey Of A Lifetime	14
Tuesday	The Butterfly Is New	16
Wednesday	Blinders Of Faith and Trust	18
Thursday	Speak To Me	21
Friday	A Gift	23
Saturday	Write Me A Letter	25
Sunday	The Line Of Love	27
Sunday Praise	Endless Joy	29

WEEK 2

Monday	Look To My Example	34
Tuesday	Of Churches And Prayers	38
Wednesday	The Gospel Of Truth	40
Thursday	Unity Of Purpose	43
Friday	Harmony	46
Saturday	The Marketplace Of Life	49
Sunday	The Manner Of Service	52
Sunday Praise	You Are My Everything, Lord	56

WEEK 3

Monday	A Conqueror, A King	60
Tuesday	To Win The Race	63
Wednesday	In The Light	67

Thursday	Facets Of The Heart	71
Friday	If You Let Me	73
Saturday	Be Diligent	75
Sunday	If You Look	77
Sunday Praise	The Gentle Rain	79

WEEK 4

Monday	It Is Simple	82
Tuesday	Windows	85
Wednesday	What You Are Is What God Sees	87
Thursday	Those Who Listen Are Satisfied	89
Friday	I Live Today	92
Saturday	God's Hunger	94
Sunday	Channels Of Love	97
Sunday Praise	The One Of Love	99

WEEK 5

Monday	Your Choice	102
Tuesday	Purified As In A Furnace	104
Wednesday	A New Awakening	106
Thursday	Many Lessons, Many Places	109
Friday	Seek More Diligently	111
Saturday	God's Answer	113
Sunday	Prayers Of The Heart	116
Sunday Praise	Small Understandings	118

WEEK 6

Monday	His Call Of Love	122
Tuesday	As God Would Have It	124

Wednesday	Travel Onward	127
Thursday	This Schoolroom	129
Friday	Stones Of Burden	132
Saturday	I Work Good In All Things	135
Sunday	My Gifts Are Yours From The Beginning	137
Sunday Praise	In This Stillness Of Night	139

WEEK 7

Monday	Faith	142
Tuesday	My Spirit	144
Wednesday	Many Faces, One Spirit	146
Thursday	Find Me First	148
Friday	Your Direction Is To Me	151
Saturday	Find Joy In Your Walk	153
Sunday	I Wait For Your Invitation	155
Sunday Praise	The Purpose Of Our Walk	158

"I would gladly speak My word to thee, and reveal My secrets, if thou wouldst diligently observe My coming, and open to Me the door of thy heart."

> The Imitation of Christ
> Book 3, Chapter XXIV
> Thomas aKempis

Preface

Dear Reader:

I invite you to join with me on a journey. A most remarkable journey. A joyful journey. A journey that Jesus opened to us two thousand years ago. He leads the journey. We are all asked to join with Him on this road to His paradise.

Your journey can begin today and it can continue for your lifetime, from this lifetime into the next. All that it requires is your joining in a daily communion with God. Many have journeyed with Him. Many are now journeying with Him. Many are being invited to begin their journey with this book. As you journey daily you will find that God will be with you moment by moment and you shall join with Him moment by moment. It is what God seeks. It is the way God is.

Jesus calls to each one of us. He knocks loudly on the door of our heart. It is sometimes difficult for us to find the key that will open the door. I believe that the key is in listening for His voice and responding to Him. Once the key is found and the door is opened He will enter into your house, dwelling with you, and teaching you daily lessons of that which He will want you to know.

Your daily lesson will become a daily communion with God for you will find that you can easily speak to Him, telling Him of your joys, your sorrows, your struggles, and He will respond by listening to you, by answering your needs, and by granting you gifts of both the spirit and the flesh. He will lift you above yourself.

I invite you now to search for the key that is in your heart for surely Jesus is knocking on the door of your heart, and surely He has lessons that He wishes to speak to you. You might begin this joyful journey by sharing daily in that which Jesus teaches us, then in prayer and meditation listen for what He will say directly to you. It will be much the same as you will read in this book and that you have heard before, for His message is the same for two thousand years. But He will speak it in those special words and in that special comfort that Jesus has just for you.

What you read in this book are daily lessons that Jesus has given me during our communion time of the last ten years. They are class notes which I diligently wrote down, for what Jesus teaches us is the most important part of our lives and guides us in our journey.

These next seven weeks can be the beginning of your journey, a beginning of your search for Him, a beginning of a daily communion with Him. The journey ends in Him, for as surely as Jesus knocks on the door of your heart to dwell with you, you shall find yourself knocking on the door of His heart to dwell with Him. All of this is done through the Trinity of God's Person for while God brings about His plan, Jesus acts in His Person and is the Gate to His Presence, and God's voice and strength is carried by His Spirit. All three are one in calling us to Him.

Each lesson in this book is complete in itself and should be meditated upon until your heart is at rest with it. You may need to, or want to, re-read the lesson allowing the words to become a part of you. I have added my own thoughts to share with you as we journey together, but these can be dispensed with if you so choose, for nothing should interfere with the words that God speaks to us directly.

If you should require more than these seven weeks to find the key of your heart then read the lessons again, or call upon me and I shall provide you with seven weeks more, and again, and again, until the key is found and you hear His voice with the ears of your own heart.

If you can hear my voice as you read these words then surely you are hearing Jesus knocking and calling your name.

Robert

A Daily Prayer

Father,
    I offer You
    this day in my life.
This life that You have given me,
    this day that You have given me.
That whatever good shall come from my life
    this day
    shall add to Your glory
        and to Your glory alone.

And, Father,
    I offer to You also
    my sins and offenses of this day
That through Jesus Christ
    I am forgiven,
    brought through salvation,
        and delivered into Your Presence,
        for all eternity.
Amen.

WEEK 1

Monday	The Journey Of A Lifetime
Tuesday	The Butterfly Is New
Wednesday	Blinders Of Faith And Trust
Thursday	Speak To Me
Friday	A Gift
Saturday	Write Me A Letter
Sunday	The Line Of Love
Sunday Praise	Endless Joy

WEEK 1
Monday

The Journey Of A Lifetime

> "... And he went ... teaching, and journeying ..."
> Luke 13:22 KJV

The journey of a lifetime. Yes. The journey with Me is truly the journey of a lifetime. Beyond your imagining. I teach as I journey. The ones who journey with Me therefore learn the secrets of My heart. They find joy in what they learn and they find joy in the progress they make in a new lifetime with Me.

I invite you to a journey which begins now, at this time, in this place with My words. Many have begun and gained a great distance. Many have yet to begin. Many will now begin.

I tell those who listen to rejoice. For My words are the words of life. Much will appear strange and beyond comprehension. But believe, and the joy of belief surpasses reason. Does the infant reason that the people before him are his parents, that they will provide for him, and therefore he should find joy in their presence? No. He simply knows joy in their presence and in his beginning journey with them. There will be time to ponder their relationship as growing and learning increase.

So be My infant. Find joy in My presence and begin your journey with Me. There will be time for pondering and learning as you progress.

This is the journey of a lifetime. There is none other like it. For it is essential to you. Those who would be with Me must journey with Me. That has been My message. And that shall be My message. It is in My very purpose.

Your moments shall be lived in peace and comfort. Your problems and worries shall be dealt with through the love of My message and not through anger or anxiety.

There is a better way to live. It is gained by stepping forth in belief and growing in faith and in trust. You are not alone, therefore you need never be alone. It is your choice.

You must make a commitment. A very direct commitment. It is made by abandoning yourself and looking to Me for your very life. A commitment of the heart. A step of faith.

In committing yourself to Me you also commit yourself to yourself. For it is your very being, your spirit, that journeys with Me. From within do you journey. From within do you learn. From within do you gain the new life. Eternal life. Different than you now know. Therefore it can only be gained through belief and faith in that belief.

Then look to Me and believe in Me. The journey of faith then begins.

On this first day of our journey it might be best to meditate on the words of this first Lesson. Know that your journey will bring you to peace, a daily peace. There is no need to rush ahead. Take each day as the only moment before you. Don't worry about tomorrow but take today and today's lesson and learn well from it. Be in quiet and peacefulness with Jesus. Listen for His voice. Hear what He will say to you. Perhaps He will simply sit beside you. Perhaps He will hold your hand. Sit in stillness and ask Jesus to visit with you. Rest with Him awhile.

You might perhaps conclude your communion time by reading from the scriptures and offering God a prayer of praise and thanks.

WEEK 1
Tuesday

The Butterfly Is New

". . . I have food to eat that you know nothing about."
John 4:32 NIV

Listen. Listen intently. And often. As you draw closer to Me our conversations will enable you to have confidence in your decisions. Your conviction will grow.

Any hesitation is a mortal feeling only. Fear of failure and fear of rejection are man's fears and are taught from generation to generation.

Withdraw then from the flesh and grow in the spirit. The spirit has confidence and understanding, for the spirit is of God, and is taught by the Holy Spirit of God.

Look within then to your spirit. Let your body be only the conveyance of your spirit. And continue your spirit in our daily conversations and in prayer and praise to your God.

I had stated at Jacob's Well that I had food that My followers did not know of. The communion of the spirit with God is the food that will sustain you. Feed yourself from within. The growth of the spirit is what is important. The body is temporal and causes too much distraction for its insignificance.

Come to Me My beloved for your sustenance. Let the Holy Spirit fill you with the food of heaven. Your health in the spirit will be pleasing to your Father. Decisions will be spontaneous. They will require little thought. For God knows all things, and imparts His knowledge through His Holy Spirit.

Be open, My beloved. Do not worry about being unworthy. Be as a child. As a child learns to walk and to talk, he trusts his parents completely. He has no fear of embarrassment of failure. Then be as a child.

Look to your heavenly Parent, your Father God for your needs, for your guidance, for your instructions. And I am of the Father and shall speak your directions.

A child, My beloved. The trust and love of a child. Simple, unstructured, fresh, new. Uncluttered by the fears of adulthood, by the harmful lessons of the evils of mankind.

A fresh new child, My beloved. Trusting and loving. Present yourself as such to your Father, and your joy will increase a thousandfold.

Let there be peace in your heart. Shed the uncertainties and restrictions of the past. You are a new person, as the butterfly is new. Emerge then in the beauty and brilliance of the spirit. Begin your new life in full flight to the Lord, your God. Let your direction be the presence of God. Venture with Me into a new spirit of knowledge and understanding.

Continue on. Continue in the spirit, continue in love. Continue to seek Me and your direction shall be made known.

Jesus says much in the simple words of this lesson. He asks us to draw near to Him and to trust in Him. He counsels us that we are to grow in the spirit and to have communion with Him as spirit to Spirit. Our communion will be our daily sustenance of the spirit. He asks us to be trusting, as a child is trusting. We can do this and as we do we shall emerge as a new child of God. We shall be a new person, "as the butterfly is new." Dwell on these words of Jesus and hold a quiet and loving communion with Him.

You might conclude your communion time by reading the scriptures and offering our loving God a prayer of praise and thanks for being with you.

Week 1
Wednesday
Blinders Of Faith And Trust

"Wisdom will save you from the ways of wicked men . . . who leave the straight paths to walk in dark ways . . ."

Proverbs 2:12, 13 NIV

Beloved, keep your direction always toward the Lord. Keep your eyes ever cast in His direction. Look not right or left. For the world lies all about you, and to look right or left will cause you to stray from your path.

Once your path is set you should not deviate. For this is reprehensible. When once you have sight of your Lord you must not lose it again, for I seek you unto Myself.

I am grieved when I am without you. From the beginning My Father gave unto Me creation and the life of man. And in this, the spirit of man is sent to earth and I grow lonely until that spirit is returned to Me. But it must be so according to My Father's will, but nonetheless, your Lord loves you and sadly misses you and awaits your return.

And to this end I speak again that when you do finally cast your eyes to Me then never look away. Set your direction in the line of your sight.

Be firm in your conviction. Have resolution in your spirit and in your flesh. Let your spirit lead your way and let your flesh follow. And let your spirit grow in strength and let your flesh diminish in strength. Be constant in this

Let My countenance be ever before you and progress in your life toward Me.

The world calls you about, of this I know. And your mortal flesh succumbs to the call. But be not deterred. Keep ever constant. As you begin to fall, seek immediately to regain your balance. If you do fall, rise immediately and continue toward Me.

If you step on a thorn, do not stop in self-pity to remove it, but continue in step and remove it as you walk. For each time that you stop, Satan calls to you. He asks you to turn your head toward him for a glimpse of his pleasures. And thus you will fall prey to his desires. And you may be lost in your journey to your Lord.

So take on yourself blinders. Place them to the side of each eye. Let one blinder be faith, and the second blinder be trust. And once secured, they shall protect you from the visions offered by Satan of the pleasures of his wickedness.

Then move constantly toward Me, and you shall see as you progress the Light that is My life and the warmth that is My love. And the more that you look directly at Me, the brighter shall be the Light and the warmer shall be the love.

The blinders of faith and trust will keep your sight in the direction of your Lord. And you will be good not to question what others would label as restraints. For the blinders are not restraints but they are strengths to keep you safe in the path of God and away from the lure of evil. These blinders will turn into wings of an angel.

Heed these lessons. Keep each word in your heart. Let the growing strength of your spirit blend into your flesh. And let your flesh turn from evil to good. And develop a full faith and trust.

I am the one Person who shall never lead you astray. Nor shall I ever condemn you. Nor shall I ever turn from you.

Keep straight in your Lord. Keep with you the happiness of your Lord. Have faith in Me. Trust in Me.

Here are words to live our life by. Can we do it? Can we put on blinders and keep our eyes fixed on Jesus? There certainly are many temptations to either side of us. Can we avoid them? It will take great strength and determination to avoid them. Blinders will surely help. Can we wear them? Will we constantly be wondering what we are missing?

The blinders of faith and trust will keep us looking ahead to where Jesus is before us. Take them in your hand and place them on yourself. You cannot ask God to do this for you. You must do it. He will help with His strength and His grace. But it is your task to do.

Praise and thanks are like faith and trust, they go hand in hand. Praise God by blessing Him and thanking Him for His goodness.

WEEK 1
Thursday

Speak To Me

". . . . when you pray, go into your room, close the door and pray to your Father . . ."
                                                Matthew 6:6 NIV

My beloved, I bring to you the task of hearing Me, communing with Me, and immersing yourself in the simplicity of finding your Lord. It is simple, yet requires strength.

To be born again in My Spirit is the simple act of prayer in acknowledging yourself as a sinner, rejecting those sins and the evil that causes sin, and in accepting your Lord Jesus as your Lord and Savior, accepting Him as He brought salvation to mankind from the penalty of sin.

A simple prayer and act of faith in asking Me to come to you and to touch your spirit, to live in your heart, will bring that to pass.

Have strength My children, to reject yourself and to accept Me. For I am your life. I am your salvation. Without My hand to bring you to the Father you shall die in your flesh.

Look to yourself for your own pursuit of salvation. Others cannot provide for you. Some will show you the way but you cannot allow others to speak for you. You must believe to yourself, in your own heart, and speak to Me in your own voice.

I will hear you. Do not think yourself unworthy to speak directly to Me. You were not unworthy that I gave My life for you. Understand that. I suffered and died for each of My Father's creations. None is unworthy.

Reach out to Me and I will reach out to you. I am reaching out to you at this very moment, why else would you be reading these words? Pray your own prayer. Speak to Me in your own words. I am the Lord your God and I will understand every utterance. You need speak only with your heart. You need not shout or be audible. For I can read your heart.

Oh My beloved child, I seek only to bring you the warmth of your God's love. You may keep your love with Me to yourself and secret as some of Mine do. You need not stand in the street and proclaim your love in a loud voice. But only speak to Me in private, quietly in your heart. And in that quietness I shall enter your heart, and dwell within you. My child, what peace you will know. What love you will know.

Come to Me then. Be refreshed. Come to life. Join Me in My life with the Father. I speak to you in love, speak to Me then in love. Now. At this very moment. Speak to Me.

Jesus speaks very directly. And He speaks simply. He asks that you speak to Him directly. See Him as a person, as a friend. Others cannot speak for you. Only you know what is in your heart. Jesus asks that you speak from your heart. Reach out to Him. Pray your own prayer. You will find yourself filled with His peace, filled with His love. Don't be timid, for no one loves you as Jesus loves you. Speak to Him.

As His peace rests with you, you might close your communion time by offering God a prayer of praise and thanks.

WEEK 1
Friday

A Gift

"So if the Son sets you free, you will be free indeed."
John 8:36 NIV

Take this freedom that I offer you. Be free. For this grace of God is meant for all who will accept it.

There are many who will not accept this freedom, but they would rather labor under their burdens. What foolishness. For I came to earth to free the sinner. I ate and drank with the sinners, with the unhealthy, to bring God's grace upon them.

A gift. A precious gift. Why will you not freely accept it? I came to free the world not to enslave it. But you would rather be slaves. You heap upon yourselves laws and regulations, each one adding a link to a long and heavy chain.

Live freely and in love and you need none but God's law. Love your neighbor as yourself. Cast out evil and welcome good, and you shall love your neighbor as yourself. Then free yourself of the burdensome regulations.

How can you proceed to God when you weigh yourself down with chains of guilt, chains of chastisement, chains of reparation?

Come. I welcome you. Each sinner. Each priest. Each neighbor. Eat with Me. Drink with Me. Dwell with Me. Leave your chains behind. Leave your brick walls behind.

Enter into this new life unburdened. Let your heart fly and be free. You need not wait for anyone else. I am your companion. I am your destination. I am your freedom.

I don't know about you but these words are certainly for me, for I have weighed myself down with tons of chain. I have tied myself to sins which have prevented me from taking even the first step in the path of Jesus. But by His goodness, Jesus teaches us another way. He teaches us that He has provided salvation for our sins. He ate and drank with sinners and so too does He eat and drink with me, a sinner. But He has accepted my burden and lifted it from me. I am free in the eternal love of God. I continue to be a sinner for I shall never in this world be perfect, but the Perfect One dwells within Me. Of this I am certain. And it is He that shall someday bring me to His perfection. Are His words not wonderful, as is His love?

I offer eternal praise and thanks to my God who loves me even in my sinfulness.

WEEK 1
Saturday

Write Me A Letter

> "... people should realize that what we are in our letters when we are absent, we will be in our actions when we are present."
>
> 2 Corinthians 10:11 NIV

Beloved, I desire that you be with Me each day. I desire this for each and every person in all places. There is so much time for many other things, but there is nothing more important to you than your God.

Each day. Spend time with Me each day. Practice it in your heart. Make it a habit of your day, like washing your face. Make it necessary to your life, like eating your food.

You will still be about your life, as you must be, but bring Me into prominence in your life.

Find Me in the way that you can understand, then keep Me with you in that manner. Pray or speak with Me. Write Me a letter. Sing a song of praise. Join with others in praise.

Find your way to communicate with Me. I am here desiring daily communion with you. If you will listen I will tell you which manner of communion is best for you.

Seek it out. Be diligent and yet be patient. When you find your voice with Me you shall know joy and contentment. And be with Me each day in your communion. Speak out to Me. And reach out to Me. You shall never know a more loving or a more constant companion. Reach out — I am here.

Write Me a letter. Write one each day. Tell Me what is in your heart. And store these letters each day. In a short while you shall be surprised at all that was in your heart to be said.

Many have difficulty in finding words to speak. So write Me a letter. Pour out your heart to Me. Your words shall be a scripture of praise to Me.

Beloved, break loose from traditions that bind you. I am your Lord. I am here for each one. Find me in your daily walk. Seek into your heart for Me.

Find the way that is best for you to communicate with Me and I will hear you. And as you open yourself in this manner you shall begin to know My response. You shall know that I am with you. You shall know a new joy.

Jesus surely understands us. He knows how easily we are distracted in our prayer time, in our communion time. But Jesus knows the solution, and He offers it to us. The only way to keep the flesh obedient to the spirit is to keep it occupied in the things of the spirit. That's not so easily done most of the time. But in our communion time and in our prayers we can keep from being distracted by writing our lessons, writing our prayers. The flesh then must follow the spirit.

Jesus suggests that we write Him a letter. Words flow more easily and we are not so easily distracted. Try it. Write a note to Jesus. Write what is in your heart. Tell Him of your joys, your struggles, your problems, and your sorrows. God wants to hear. Write to Him as you would to a parent, to a brother or sister, or to a friend. As you write, He listens. You might then also write as you listen to what He speaks to you.

Take pencil and paper in hand and begin to write daily. Let the words flow. And capture them on paper so that you might store them in your private room, and perhaps you may eventually share them with others.

You might take the time to re-read today's lesson before beginning your writing. You might also write your prayer of praise and thanks to Him. Nothing elaborate — just very simple, even if you only write "I Love You."

WEEK 1
Sunday

The Line Of Love

". . . he drew me out of deep waters."
Psalm 18:16 NIV

Many, my beloved, are adrift in the world. They are filled with fear and anxiety as if swimming alone in dark deep water. How alone and fearful is that person who looks about and sees no one to help him.

But look further, those who are adrift in the deep water. Look to the shore. I am on that shore. On My shore of safety I have the line of life, the line of love, in My hand. I have one line for each person who is born. Their name is on the line and I know them.

As I tug the line, a word of love reaches their heart, and as I do this the more their heart stirs and they know that I am calling them. The person who reads these words will know whether I am tugging on their line at this instant or not. They will feel a slight stirring in their heart for Me. They will sense the slightest feeling of joy and comfort.

This first day, this first sensation, means that I am here and I am calling you. Throughout the days and the nights now, your heart will not let you forget that it is your time, that your Lord brings His love to you now. You can begin to seek the shore. The deep water does not bother you any longer for you know that you will be saved by My hand.

From this point, read more words. Learn of Me the more. Begin to trust in Me, and in yourself. I am your Lord. I am a loving Lord. I will use no tricks to bring you to Me. I will use only the line of love which I keep tied to you. As you feel Me pull on that line you can hasten your return to the shore of My love if you will begin to pull on your end of the line also.

For ours will be a sharing love. As I love you, you will return My love. As I abide in you, you shall abide in Me.

So reach now for the line of love that is tied to you. Search for it — it is within your heart. When you find it, it will have the name of Jesus on it. Hold it fast within your heart, and as I gently pull you to Me, let your heart pull Me to you. Slowly. Evenly. With love.

How beautifully Jesus expresses His concern for us. We are tied to Him with a line of love. We are safe. We need not be troubled. We need but find this line of love — it is in our heart. We need but call the Name of Jesus and He responds — that is our line of love. He responds by calling our name. And our heart finds a new peace. A new comfort. A new love. The line of love. Jesus has this line tied to each one of us. We are His if we choose to be. Find Him and deliver yourself to Him on this journey.

Tie the line of love fast by reading from the scriptures, and by offering God a prayer of praise and thanks as often as possible.

WEEK 1
Sunday Praise

Endless Joy

Precious Lord,
   in the quietness of this time,
   and in the stillness of this person
   the feeling of joy swells within me.
For i know that You are with me.
i need only look within,
   and there You are.
Always there.
No matter what my mood or disposition.

i am not bursting with joy as a person today.
i feel quiet,
   and a little withdrawn.
That is my face to the world.
But yet i need only turn my attention within myself
   and there i am overwhelmed with joy.
For there,
   is a marching band,
   a heavenly choir,
   a symphony orchestra,
   shouting children,
   thousands of voices raised in praise.
There within, my Lord,
   is You.

How happy i am.
How comforted i am.
How joyous i am.

My spirit leaps for joy.
It is probably best that this joy is contained within,

        for if i were to act according to my joy
        then i would be as a romping,
        noisy lunatic.
For if i would act on the outside
        as i feel within
        then i would fly at lightning speed
        around the earth
        a thousand times,
        and light up the sky with endless rainbows,
        and bursting stars,
        and showers of fireworks.
For i have enough joy within me
        that i could light up the world.
And this joy is You my Lord.
This joy is Your love,
        Your most Holy Spirit.
This joy is the presence of my God.
Thank You Lord.
Thank You for Your saving grace.
Thank You for Your presence.
Thank You for Your endless joy.

Some may find it difficult at first to praise God directly. Most of us have reserved that place for religious leaders thinking perhaps that only those appointed ones, priests, ministers, clerics are endowed with the ability and authority to offer praises to God. But did your own parent not glow and appreciate any word of acknowledgement and love that you offered them? God is our parent. We as His children can look directly at Him, and speak directly to Him of our love and praise of Him. We are His children. He has an equal love for us as He does for any evangelist, priest, minister, nun, monk — any dedicated servant.

God wants us to understand this. All of these teachings lead us to this point. Our God is a loving God. He loves each one of us and seeks communion with each one of us. And as our loving Parent He seeks to know our response to Him. He seeks to read our heart.

It is important that we form these words in our heart. Words of praise. Words of thanks. Words of recognition that all that we are, all that we have, is through the grace of God.

The scriptures are filled with praise of God and so are our hearts filled with praise. We need but form the words within. Express them within. Speak them or whisper them if you are able to. If not, simply dwell in silence on God's goodness to us and to your love for Him.

WEEK 2

Monday	Look To My Example
Tuesday	Of Churches And Prayers
Wednesday	The Gospel Of Truth
Thursday	Unity Of Purpose
Friday	Harmony
Saturday	The Marketplace Of Life
Sunday	The Manner Of Service
Sunday Praise	You Are My Everything, Lord

WEEK 2
Monday

Look To My Example

"Bear with each other and forgive whatever grievances you may have against one another."
Colossians 3:13 NIV

    Beloved, I know of the desire of many in their heart to serve Me. For when I walked the earth I had a strong desire to serve My Father. And those who desire will serve as I served. But you must be patient as was necessary for Me.

    It was for Me to be born an infant and to grow into maturity before I could properly serve My purpose. And so it must be for you also.

    A spirit who is born again in Me is but an infant. And that infant must grow to maturity before it is strong enough and learned enough to fulfill its purpose. It requires patience, but this is an exercise in humility and will temper you for your service.

    God, My Father, is the Perfect Being. For you to choose to attain His presence is no easy task. For you must climb from the depths of the flesh to the brilliance of the spirit. But it is possible. And not only possible, but God Himself helps you through My Being. For that is My purpose.

    It required thirty years of My life on earth to reach My maturity for My purpose. It may take you that long to gain maturity of the spirit for your service to God. Let patience and understanding be before your eyes and in your heart during your growing years.

    Look to My example. Look to My life. You will see that I grew as a child among My family. And I enjoyed friends and I worked among them. And so you must do the same. Grow in the presence of your family. And make friends, and work.

As you grow in your spiritual life renew yourself with your family. Make them as new friends. For in the flesh, families grow apart, while new friends are welcomed as fresh and new without fault. The reason is that you have come to know too well the faults of your brothers and sisters, and you have had to live with those faults. And each of them had to live with your faults. And the same with your parents. And so a distance grows between you because the flesh seeks to avoid the faults in others and dislikes being reminded of its own faults.

So the flesh seeks new friends whose faults are unknown. And amongst them you can hide your own faults. But this is pride. This is not love.

So in your zeal to love Me and to serve Me, I tell you that as a new Christian and growing spirit in God, you must turn these things of the flesh to the things of the spirit.

Look to those in your family and renew your love with them. Look at their faults and love them for their faults, for each person in your family is a person in God. And you do not know his or her place with God. And they do not know yours.

So open your eyes and your heart in love for them. If you cannot be a Christian to your brothers and sisters then you cannot be a Christian to others. And even more with your parents. For they have borne the labor of your childhood and lived the responsibility of your growing years. They have served in this, their purpose.

Yes, your first act in My Name is to renew your love with your family. And be supportive, for all may not be born again in the spirit. Thus, must you be patient and humble, for your purpose is now in God, while theirs may not yet be.

In this you can measure your humility and patience. Let this be your measuring stick. For you must accomplish this in your heart before you can accomplish any more.

Forgive others their faults to the depths in your heart and seek forgiveness for your faults. This is the learning for your infancy and growing years in Me. This is your purpose as a newborn in Me.

When your heart is pure and unshackled from the resentments of the flesh, then shall you be able to see My footprints. Then shall you be able to look at Me and say "Lord, Lord, I desire to serve you."

There is more to searching within yourself than finding Me, for you must search even deeper to find yourself.

When you find Me you are saved. When you find yourself you are in the path to the Presence of God. For your spirit must be cleansed and purified. Your spirit dies to be born again in Me.

Yes, My beloved, I know of your eagerness to serve Me. But first grow in the spirit. Cleanse and renew yourself.

It is not an easy search nor an easy task to perform. But I am here with you and the Holy Spirit moves about to bestow His powers upon you as you require them.

My world is of beauty. My world is magnificent as befits the Spirit of God. Look toward my world. Know that it exists and know that a place is here for you.

With all your heart, love others as you love Me. See Me in others for I am there. See Me in your parents. See Me in your brothers and sisters and they shall see Me in you.

Proceed then My loved one. Do this for Me. For My honor. And for My glory.

Is it not true with all of us that as we discover our love for God that we desire to rush headlong into any service toward Him that enters our mind? But Jesus cautions us to have patience. He asks us to search within and to begin to live within. He asks us to look at His life with His family and friends. We are to do the same. We are to begin our journey with Him by renewing our love with our parents and family. Healing our hearts and growing within is essential to finding the peace that Jesus offers us. Our roots must be strong. Renew and revitalize your roots. Reaffirm your childhood. Look to those who have helped you and supported you in the past, in your childhood. This may appear to be very difficult for some, but God's love is with us and shall be our strength. If those from our past have left this life then the renewing can be in the spirit. For surely, by the teachings of Jesus, our spirits live on, and spirit knows spirit. Follow Jesus. Follow where His love will lead you.

Pray for parents and family, those near and dear, and those separated by distance or by differences of our personalities. Grow as a new infant, a new person in God. Grow with a pure and forgiving heart.

Offer God a prayer of praise and thanks. Bless Him every moment.

WEEK 2
Tuesday

Of Churches And Prayers

"For where two or three come together in my name, there am I with them."
Matthew 18:20 NIV

My beloved, know that the Spirit of your Lord is moving over the earth, and that according to My Father's will, and in My Father's time, the end of the road will be reached when all people will know, and My Father's plan shall be accomplished. But, my beloved, it is far from that time yet. It is far. Much is being done by many, in service, in praying, in spreading the Good News to their neighbors. Yes, much is being done but much much more work remains.

It is as the chimneys of winter when you were a child, my beloved. Do you remember that as a child you looked about during the winter and wondered how winter could continue with its grasp when so many chimneys were sending heat into the air? You stood and looked so often at the chimneys but yet you saw the cold winter remain about you. How could this be, you thought? Surely the heat from the chimneys will accumulate and cancel the effects of winter. But they did not.

And so now today you wonder why the chimneys of the many church services and gatherings in My Name do not melt the coldness of the world, why the prayers of the chimneys do not accumulate to drive away Satan and let warmth settle on the land.

My beloved, the chimneys of the churches and gatherings are serving a purpose just as were the chimneys of the homes that you counted as a child. The chimneys serve as a signal that there is heat within the home and that people are being warmed and preserved by the fire within.

And so it is with the many church services, and indeed each such prayer of praise from any lips in any gathering that utter the name of God. Prayers are the heat that will warm and preserve God's people through their time away from Him. And the churches and gatherings are the chimneys that give indication of the warmth of prayer that is inside.

But yes, no matter how many chimneys there are, winter will continue to live, the cold will still visit you. Chimneys will not overcome totally the strength of nature.

And so it is with prayer. Your prayer will serve its necessary purpose to keep alive those who dwell near the fire of your Lord, but it is only when I return to earth as the Son of Man, that winter will be overcome. Only the power of your Father can overcome. Do not look for it in any other quarter.

Continue heating your hearts and counting the chimneys. Continue in your prayers and count the churches. But stoke the furnace of your hearts, all you who read. For some chimneys, even though they stand, are cold. The only chimneys to be counted are those that send up heat, rising to the heavens.

Feed the flames with your prayers of love. The Son of Man waits near, to melt the evil of Satan and bring the freshness of springtime to all people. And when the winter is blown away into oblivion, the warmth of the Father, greater than all the summers of the universe, will envelop you and carry you to eternal life in the bosom of your Lord.

Prayer is communion with God. It need not be a ritual. It can be very simple. Speak to God and listen for His reply. His reply might only be stillness and a peaceful quietness within. But surely He does reply. Simply be with Him. You need not even speak words but only direct your thoughts and yourself toward Him. He will know, He will listen, and He will be with you. Pray from the heart, simply. Take your time. Be still.

You might conclude this communion time by reading the scriptures and offering a prayer of praise and thanks.

WEEK 2
Wednesday

The Gospel Of Truth

"If you hold to my teaching, you are really my disciples. Then you will know the truth, and the truth will set you free."

John 8:31, 32 NIV

These words are the gospel of Truth. For I am the Truth. And I am the same of God as was begotten, as lived and died on earth for you, and who lives in the world today in the hearts of those who believe in Me.

I am not a God of confusion or of contradiction. I speak but one truth — this never changes. But for you to understand the full truth and the meaning of My words you must receive many lessons. If you receive only a small number of lessons, then there will be many questions in your heart. But if you receive many, and continuing lessons, then your questions will disappear.

My lessons during My life on earth were sufficient to begin My church and to continue it. But now that My time draws near again for Me to be with you, I desire that all will find a fuller knowledge of Me so that they may welcome their God in full knowledge and understanding of who He is.

I speak words that will bring you to Me. For I am already with you.

As you come to know Me and believe in Me, so then shall you seek Me within your heart. I speak words of truth and not of condemnation. I speak words of love and not of judgment. Those things that shall be in the judgment, shall be. But it is more necessary now that you come to know your Lord. It is more necesary that you come to life in your Lord.

My call goes out to all people of earth, for My Spirit is with all people of earth. Mighty shall be the signs of My coming. But before that, I shall speak in the whisper of these words, so that you will know that I am of love and not of fear.

I speak in the whisper of these words so that your heart will open in love and not in trembling. In these words find yourself, and find Me.

Seek within your heart to find the person that you are — the person of the spirit and of the flesh. And seek within your heart to find Me, for I am with you.

When you come to know this, you shall hear My voice. And you shall be free. For the truth of My words shall make you free. You shall throw off your burdens in rejoicing. You shall know that you have a place with your Lord. Nothing is more important to you, and nothing should be put before this.

The words of love and the words of truth. Listen to them, and you shall be born again. Listen to them, and your spirit shall live.

The Gospel of Truth — My words of Truth. Receive them in truth and you shall be made whole — a person in the balance of the spirit with the flesh.

I love you as My children. I seek only to gather you to Me as the storm approaches. I seek to envelop you, to protect you. I seek to give you shelter.

What parent does not yearn for a lost child? What parent will not protect his child from danger? Know then that I am your parent, your father and mother, your Lord and Savior, and you are My child.

And I do yearn for you, and I shall protect you. But you must come to know this so that it will happen. You must come to know the heart of your Lord. And this you can do through My words.

Heed My words, all that I say. I speak to each one, I speak to many, and I speak to all. There are no contradictions, there are only many different lessons for many different persons.

Read My lessons and know which ones are for you. I shall lead you to them. And you shall know in your heart which lessons are for you.

Not all lessons are for all who read these words. But find your lessons and learn by them. Find your lessons, believe them, live by them, and you shall find Me. And when you find Me, you find your life. When you find Me, you find the Love of God.

Believe this, know that it is true. Be not conscious of the means by which you receive these words, but only that they are from the right hand of God. And the truth of My words shall set you free.

Your communion time with God is a time when you step out of your world and into that private place where you and God join together as one. He speaks the words of His truth to you. Be as His child at this time. Listen as He teaches, as He counsels. Tell Him of your uncertainties, your problems, and allow Him as your loving Parent to guide you and to assist you.

He speaks words of truth and not of condemnation. He speaks words of love and not of judgment. He speaks in whispers so that your heart will know no fear but will respond in whispers of love.

Let us offer God a prayer of praise for His presence, for the truth of His words, for this outpouring of His love to each one of us.

WEEK 2
Thursday

Unity Of Purpose

". . . that ye may attend upon the Lord without distraction."

1 Corinthians 7:35 KJV

Beloved, in your endeavor to follow your path, strive to have a unity of purpose. For in directing your efforts in unity there will be an increase in progress and you will be less susceptible to distraction. For it is easy for distraction to mount when your purpose is divided.

The branches of a tree sway in the wind for there are many of them and they are small in size. But the trunk of the tree is solid and has great strength for it embodies all the energy of each branch.

In your efforts then, be as the trunk of the tree. Gather all of your energy into one purpose, a unified purpose. And that unity of purpose shall have great strength.

And direct that unity of purpose to life with your Lord. Keep this direction and you shall not fail in your task. And your heart shall know much joy. For in your Lord is much joy. And you shall find happiness within yourself, for through your dedication shall your flesh serve your spirit. And when your flesh does submit to the spirit, then shall you find completeness.

As you progress it is not sufficient to merely ward off the distractions that act upon you. For in warding off the distractions you simply repel them but you do not win a victory over them. They shall return.

What is necessary is that you tear from your flesh that part that is the target of your distractions. Remove the target and the distractions shall find no mark. And in that portion of flesh that is removed shall enter the growth of the spirit and you shall continue to be whole, and your wholeness shall enter into the spirit rather than the flesh.

Thus it was spoken that if your hand offends, then cut it off; if your eyes offend, gouge them out. My lesson was to tear out, in spirit, that part of the flesh that offends. Remove it in your heart and in your mind as the target of distraction and as the cause of offense.

Pray for the strength of your spirit to replace that flesh with the goodness of the Spirit of God. Endeavor to bring a spiritual completeness to your person to replace the evil parts of flesh.

And it is different for each person, for each person is different, one from the other. What offends in one person does not offend in the next person. Thus it is that you should seek within yourself to know yourself, to seek out that part of the flesh that offends. To tear from your heart and your mind that part of the flesh that causes the offense and is subject to distraction from your purpose.

Tear from yourself those distractions as you would prune a tree to give it added strength and to direct its purpose in bearing more fruit. Thus, you see, My lessons are the same now as when I walked the earth. I have not changed.

But I send you more words of truth so that you will know Me. I send you more words of truth so that you will come to believe in Me and to believe that I am the salvation of humankind. And to believe that My purpose is to bring you to the love of God. And to believe that I am the Gate to the presence of God; that it is I who shall bring you to the Father.

My words are simple, and My words are true. Listen with your heart and you will know that My words are true. For My lessons will lead you to yourself, they will lead you to Me, and they will lead you to the Holy Spirit of God, and they will lead you to God who is the Unity of the universe, the Unity of heaven, the Unity of all who believe.

My Father shall gather to His Unity all that is good and shall disperse from his sight all that is not good.

And that which He disperses shall be flung to the far corners. But that which is good shall be brought in My hand and through My heart to His presence to share with Him the joy of eternity with Him. Praise be to God. Hallelujah!

Jesus asks us to begin a cleansing process within ourselves that we might be able to gain strength within ourselves. He tells us to be as the trunk of a tree. We should gather all of our energy into one unified purpose. And that purpose is life with God. Nothing else is important. When we find our life in God all else will follow. We sway about like the branches of a tree following every whim of this world. We seek to gain for ourselves that which only God can give us. We are to seek God first. When we are one with Him all else will fall into place, and we shall not sway about. But rather we shall have a single, solid strength which is ourselves unified with God.

Strength is gained in trust, faith, and prayer. We should at all times and in all places offer our prayers of praise and thanks to our God.

WEEK 2
Friday

Harmony

"He will call upon me, and I will answer him."
Psalm 91:15 NIV

Harmony, My beloved, harmony. All of God's world is in harmony. Can you not hear it? Can you not see it? Each action, each sound, even the discords, are in harmony.

It is God who assembled the musicians and the place. It is God who holds the baton and calls the players into action.

When you begin to see God in things that are about you, then you are beginning to receive your lessons from the Holy Spirit. In the orchestra, as all that happens is orchestrated and conducted with a plan and with diligence, you can see there God acting in His own plan. The orchestra is but a model.

For God in His majesty has assembled no less than an orchestra of His world and He has prepared the place for it to be. And He has created the players and He has composed the music that will be. And He stands before it all and through His will does He call it into action.

Over endless time does God do this. And it all changes and grows. For even man has come as a chorus at the end to add majesty and finality to God's work.

Each note, each tone is brought by God's hand and blends into the harmony of His work. Crashing sounds as well as sweet ones. Quiet moods and thunderous moods.

A person's laughter comes through God's laughter, so also does a person's music come through God's music. Not unlike, My beloved — but rather each person is in the image and likeness of God.

See it everywhere and in everything. See that God is in everything. Each experience of your moments is in God. See it this way. Those things that are about you are in God. Know it. Feel it. All in harmony.

Though you may dwell in the discord that is about, try to look beyond that to see and hear the fullness that is larger than the discord.

What wonder it is to see the plan unfold, to see the start and development of a theme, to see the counterplay and to watch the explosion of joy and satisfaction when the fullness of the moment is met.

Oh yes. It is all there. And it is there for you. It is there for your joy and for your satisfaction. See it this way. Do not stand outside and wonder what is happening inside. Hearing the thunder of harmony do you not want to see it? Do you not want to be a part of it?

Enter in then. See what is happening. Take part in it. Be one who contributes. Look to the Leader and look to be called upon. And do what you are called upon to do even though to you it is of little consequence or does not appear to be in harmony. For you do not see the fullness, but only one part.

And so when the Leader's finger points to you then do His will with all your heart for it will be in keeping with the fullness of the Master's harmony. He knows better than any the sound that must come forth. And in this must come your faith that it is good and it is right. Know that your part will be heard. It will enter into the total fullness.

Beloved, I speak in pictures many times for My lessons are not meant to be a labor; a difficult task. No, My lessons are meant to be heard in sweetness and understanding. In quietness and the relaxation of joy. For that is God's way. I do not mean to tax you or to cause you confusion. But if you desire to know your God then you will be understanding to God's ways.

God is the poet unsurpassed. God is the musician without equal. All that man is, is through the hand of God. Measure out your own talent, add it to the talents of all people who have lived, then multiply the total by an infinite number and therein you shall see the talent of God. And this talent is yours.

It is at your disposal. Through Me. This is God's will and this is God's desire.

Beloved, will you stand before Me? Will you allow Me to gather you into your proper station so that the Master Musician may call you into action? Will you be a part of the orchestra of man? Will you stand with Me when I signal My Father that all is prepared for Him? This is My task and I call upon you to be with Me in it. My Father's loving eyes watch. And He waits.

Beloved, be with Me. Join My body. Prepare yourself for action in Me. Together we shall praise God.

How can anyone not want to be a part of this orchestra of all the people of the world? We are not isolated, you and I, but we are part of God's creation and we are called to take our place in this creation. We may consider that we are the least important of all the people in this orchestra but that is God's place to know us. Remember that in God's kingdom the last shall be first. God's kingdom is the opposite of this world where we place our leaders upon thrones and pay them honor. In God's kingdom it is the servant who is honored, it is the least who is the greatest. I choose to be least. I choose to sit in a quiet corner waiting patiently for God to point His finger and say "Now, quiet servant, is your moment to join in with Me."

We are, each one, a part of God's harmony, a part of His plan, a part of His life. In your communion time find your place to stand, find the place where it is that God desires you to be. Listen closely, He will tell you exactly where He desires you to be and exactly what part He asks you to play.

While we stand and wait, while we search and listen, we can do nothing greater than to place our trust in God and to offer Him our continuing prayer of praise and thanks.

WEEK 2
Saturday

The Marketplace Of Life

". . . They are like children sitting in the marketplaces and calling out to others."
Matthew 11:16 NIV

One with you am I. We two joined in the Spirit. I know this and you must learn it. You must know it. You must feel it. Therein will be your comfort and your strength. For no matter what happens in your life, you will be secure in Me.

Do not pray to Me as if I am some distant God in His far-off heaven. But pray to Me within you. You know that your heart beats within you. Know also that I live within you.

When your mind is convinced of this and accepting of it then your life will change. Your walk in life will become as simple as a walk in the marketplace. At a leisure pace, looking about at what is offered, choosing what you care to, but never once worrying about suffering a loss.

Life is nothing more than this, the gathering of your daily bread while walking in My walk. Why make it more difficult than this?

Yes, you can scurry about as a mouse. You can worry and fret that another gathers more than you. You can stumble about drunken by the goodness that is offered. You can be fattened by gluttony to the point where you cannot move, where you cannot walk your walk. That is your responsibility.

I place you at one end of the marketplace and I tell you only that I shall meet you at the other end. How then will you walk your walk? Alone and frightened? Rebellious and antagonistic? In circles never ending? Straight and sure, taking only what you need?

Will you walk alone or will you ask Me to walk with you? Will you ask Me to lead the way?

So many become lost in the marketplace of life for no reason. They see it as a slave market rather than a gift of treasures.

What do your eyes see? What does your heart feel? Are your steps sure? Are you at a leisure pace?

Read these words and understand them. I do not choose to speak commands, to order you in each step that you take. I am a Father who takes His child for a day in the marketplace.

Do you become lost and confused? Frightened? Do you have confidence and believe that I have brought you to the marketplace for a good purpose? That I watch over you and desire only that you should benefit and find what you need as you walk in the marketplace?

There is a straight path through the length of the marketplace from the beginning to the end. Do you walk this straight path, taking only what you need to make your progress, or do you ramble about taking in your arms all that you can until it becomes a burden to carry it all?

The simple path or the burdensome path? Do you look to see Me at the end of your walk or do you know in your heart that I have not left you, but that I am at your side through your entire walk, each step of the way?

Have you seen a child lost in a marketplace because he looked about in greed and lost sight of his parent before him? The child is frightened. Are you a lost, frightened child?

Then look for Me and find Me, then keep your eyes on Me and I will lead you in safety. Call My Name and I shall come to you.

What parent knowing that their child is lost will not look for their child? Do you have faith as a child in your parent? Do you know in your heart that your parent would never abandon you, but will search for you until you are found?

Have faith then. For I am your Father and I search for you now. Are you also searching for Me? Do you call My Name as I call yours?

Beloved child. If you are lost and searching, then stand firm in strength and confidence. Stand still for a moment to determine with a clear mind who you are and where you are. Look to see where I am and look to see the path that will bring you to Me. You will see it if you look.

The more you look for Me, the closer shall I be to you. Then when you have found Me, your progress through the marketplace will be sure, and filled with the joy of reunion with your Father. What a happy time. We will rejoice at our union and we shall then walk each step together.

The marketplace will then be as the place intended. The place of your daily bread. Your place of provision. Not a place of confusion. Not a prison. But a place where I provide for you while I enact My will and you perform your purpose. Look not in the dark places, but in the light, and you shall see this.

What wonderful simplicity can be ours in living through our life in this world. Why do we make it difficult? There certainly is a noisy crowd in this marketplace of life but need we get caught up in it? Need we fill our arms with food and treasures until we can no longer move? There is more than we need in this marketplace. We need only to hear these teachings of God to know that we can live in peace and in love even though those about us are raucous and greedy.

God speaks very clearly and tells us that the manner of our walk is our responsibility. He is certainly standing next to us ready to walk with us and even to lead us. He waits for our invitation to Him. He will not place a chain around us and lead us like His slave. But He loves us. He searches for us as His lost child. He wants to be with us during our walk and to welcome us into His house at the end of our walk. Our God is a simple, loving God. We must search to know this in our hearts.

As always, we should offer our prayer of praise and thanks to this wonderful Parent who loves us so dearly.

WEEK 2
Sunday

The Manner Of Service

"If one falls down, his friend can help him up."
Ecclesiastes 4:10 NIV

Beloved, I speak of service to Me. For at times many hearts are troubled over the degree of their service. And if their hearts are directed to learning these lessons then their eyes will see more clearly with each lesson.

And perhaps you now are open to know that service to Me is not in magnificent gestures and glittering ceremonies. They are manifestations of praise but not of service.

True service to Me is as the communion which I seek with you, private and quiet, unadorned with loud announcements or life-giving sacrifices.

Service to Me is the breath that you take in My Name.

Service to Me is offering your labor of the day, your thoughts, your heartbeats.

Service to Me is the helping gesture to another. A smile of comfort to one in need, a voice of support to one in difficulty.

Service to Me is looking at another with compassion and just standing ready to help those in need.

You read glowing accounts of those who have served Me. The stories are magnificent, telling of a life of service in suffering. But that is because you see such a life in its entirety. But what do you think was the everyday life of My servant? Was every day filled with miracles and great events? No.

Try to see the lives of My servants the way they truly were. You make them saints because you have accumulated all their good deeds into one book. But had you been with them in the walk of their life you would see that their service was in many small deeds, small services.

My servants were not bowed down to, nor highly regarded in most cases. They simply walked in My path each day and lived with Me in their hearts. Their days were filled with small gestures and words of conviction. Many people turned away from them.

When you paint a house you do not wave your hand and it is finished. But rather you start by cleansing the house of stains and rotted areas. You scrape the boards clean of worn loose paint. Then stroke by stroke, with your brush you apply the paint to bring the house to newness again.

So it is with My servants. They begin with a cleansing process brought by the Holy Spirit. Then slowly, moment by moment, day by day, they take on the appearance of the new person. Stroke by stroke, service by service, they are new.

Who do you see that serves Me in one magnificent gesture? Did Paul? Or Peter? Day by day the small services are accumulated.

No one performs miracles except through the Holy Spirit. Paul did not perform a service to Me in his miracles. Nor did My apostles. But rather their dedication of daily service to Me prepared them to be a channel for the power of the Holy Spirit.

In the performance of miracles it is God who performs the service to man, not man performing a service to God. Look not then to performing miracles, for that is God's work. But look to being of service to Me in each task that you do, each day.

As is said often "every day in every way I am getting better and better," work toward, and say in direction to Me "every day in every way I am getting closer and closer."

Loving service is simple. It is direct. More of a sharing than a service.

As you look upon a house that is newly painted and see the splendor, so is it that you look upon those who have served Me in the past. You see the total task completed, but you have not witnessed the tedious cleansing and the many diligent strokes of the brush.

The strokes of the brush are the many small services performed in My Name. Unselfish, loving service. Some almost too small to mention as would the painter remove a hair pulled loose from the brush. But each service, each task, adds to the total.

See this in your own life then. Cleanse and paint your own house as did My other servants, and did My apostles.

With diligence. With countless small services. Gestures, smiles, words of comfort, prayers of faith, prayers of praise. One stroke and then another. One small service and then another. If each person did this then the whole world would be made new. What a beautiful and glorious sight that would be to Me upon My return.

I would return then not in judgment but to attend a glorious feast with My beloved. What a wonderful gift that would be of man to his God. A new world, cleansed of its stains and shining with a rainbow of color, of new life, of joy. The reward of a loving service.

Beloved, take my lessons to your heart. Learn them, study them. By My words you will learn how to cleanse yourself and to make yourself new. Do this and you will share a feast of eternal life with Me.

Love and serve your God. Love and serve your neighbor. Love and serve yourself.

With diligence, stroke by stroke, service by service are we made new. How simple and straightforward are the teachings of God. Could they be made any more simple? We seem to immerse ourselves in complex issues and rattle our brains to display our intelligence and to increase our stature over others. But God reminds us over and over that we should be childlike. Take small steps. Learn bit by bit. We are to diminish ourselves not to puff ourselves up. The cleansing process of the newly born in God is a slow, detailed process. And so is our service when once we are cleansed. Bit by bit, stroke by stroke do we become the new person. It requires much patience and diligence. But God is patient. He waits for us. And He is diligent in His waiting and in His helping.

These teachings are simple for a purpose, for God's life is simple, His love is simple, His ways are simple. The simpler we become in our thoughts and actions, the closer do we come to God and to His kingdom.

In simplicity does God seek to hear our words to Him, our prayers. He asks that you state, very simply, your needs. And He desires, very simply, that you recognize Him through your words of praise and thanks.

WEEK 2
Sunday Praise
You Are My Everything, Lord

Oh Lord,
    as i walk through my daily life
        know that You are in my heart always.
As i plod through the moments of the day
    i am lost,
        for this place is foreign to me.
    i belong with You, Lord.
        i am Your child.
Yet to reach You
    i must live here first,
        and so i shall,
    but my heart is elsewhere,
        my heart is with You.

i become more of a shadow of a being
    for i direct myself increasingly to You.
    The less that i become
        the greater Your glory
        rises within me.
If i could
    i would cast myself
    to the farthest corner
        of this universe.
    But i have heard Your word
    and Your instruction
        that i am to live here
        and am to be patient.
i am not always living.
    and i am not always patient.

But love grows —
   my love for You, Lord,
   and all else pales before You.
Forgive my transgressions, Lord.
   My sins mount up around me,
      and the hurts that i cause
      seem endless.
Yet Your love is surely with me;
i am born again,
and dwelling in my eternity
   with You.
Your lessons live with me Lord,
   and slowly i learn Your meaning.
You instruct me to be patient Lord;
   i ask that You be patient with me.
You urge me to pray, Lord;
   i cannot pray without You,
   i cannot live without You,
   i cannot die without You,
   i cannot rise to Your side without You.

You are my everything Lord,
   and i long to be with You
      as You are now with me.
i shall plod the moments of this life Lord,
   according to Your will.
But in my happiness
   my joy shall not be complete
   until that time
      when i shall gaze upon Your face
   and kneel before You
   and worship You
   and enter into Your house
      for all eternity.

Much praise is offered to God throughout the scriptures. Search and know the praises that have been offered. Then we, in our born-again spirit, can offer the praises that the Holy Spirit releases from our heart. Surely the spirit that loves God seeks to praise Him. Let us in stillness, in peace of heart, and in simplicity praise God for Himself and for His goodness.

WEEK 3

Monday	A Conqueror, A King
Tuesday	To Win The Race
Wednesday	In The Light
Thursday	Facets Of The Heart
Friday	If You Let Me
Saturday	Be Diligent
Sunday	If You Look
Sunday Praise	The Gentle Rain

WEEK 3
Monday

A Conqueror, A King

". . . the kingdom of God is within you."
Luke 17:21 NIV

Yes, it is true, I conquer in the night. I conquer in whispers of My voice. I conquer in the quietness within.

I need not raise My voice. I need not carry arrow and spear. My conquering is in the Spirit. The very Spirit of God by Whom you were born. By Whom you came to be. And by Whom you shall be in Me.

A Conqueror. A King. Yes. But rather than a King, a Brother. For I am a King in My Father, but I am a Brother in you.

Yes, beloved, look not in the halls of greatness, but look for Me within the quietness of your heart. For My work is not to be done with a loud clamor over the countryside, but My work is to be done in the quiet, in the secret places of your heart and mind. For My kingdom is not a place of palaces but My kingdom is within you. Each one.

Each one who hears Me is to Me a palace. A king. A brother, a sister. A spirit to spirits.

If you could know Me then you would know the love of God. For I am not to Myself as you would see Me, but rather I am begotten in love and for love.

Thus My conquering is not by the spear but by the word of truth. In the silence of your heart. In the still of the night. What gain would I make to conquer your flesh? For the flesh is but a flash, a spark, then it dies. But should I conquer your spirit and keep it in the confines of good and away from the destruction of evil, then all of heaven sings a joyful song. For each spirit returned to God multiplies His glory.

Thus, yes, I am a Conqueror, a King. This King conquers death. This King brings life. This King is a Gate to the Heart of God. This King is but a servant. A Son of God, yet servant to man. A King of man yet a servant to God.

God is all things to all people, and I am His right hand. I am of Him and I am with Him. And too, I am of man and with man.

If you feel conquered by Me then shout for joy, for God has your spirit within His bosom. If you feel conquered by Me then feel the strength which I bring to you. If you feel conquered by Me then feel the freedom which I bring to you.

For God does not conquer as man would conquer, but God welcomes, God gives, God accepts. When you submit to Me you will not relinquish, but you will gain. When you submit to Me you are not conquered, but rather you are freed. A strangeness to your ears perhaps, but your spirit understands. And it is your spirit that I seek. It is your spirit only that can proceed through My Gate.

Be conquered then and be My brother, My sister. Be conquered then and know My love. Be conquered then and hear God's voice call to you. In the quietness and in the stillness yield to My love and join the kingdom of God.

"Then all of heaven sings a joyful song." How important God considers each of us to be. That is the word that runs through all of these teachings. God speaks directly to each one of us if we will only take the time to listen, if we will only trust that it is so. Those who do trust know God's joy within them. It's difficult to understand but we need to reverse our understanding, for God's heaven seems to be the opposite of our world.

Jesus says, "If you feel conquered by Me then feel the freedom which I bring to you." In this world if we are conquered, then we are subservient. In God's heaven when we are conquered we are free. God's "conquering" is claiming us for

Himself. He directs Satan that we are off limits to his evil. We are a child of God. We are reborn out of evil and into God's Spirit. All of these teachings of Jesus tell us that this is so. We need but read His teachings, have faith in the truth of His words, trust that it is so, and we are then one with Him. Our communion can proceed unimpaired by the call of Satan. The blinders of faith and trust will keep us on the right path.

I personally claim Jesus as my Savior and my God in the Trinity as the one true God. I reject Satan and all that Satan is. It is a simple creed but it is all that is necessary.

Please join with me daily in reflecting on the goodness of God. Join in the deliverance of ourselves to Him and to Him alone. Joy increases as evil decreases. As we draw nearer to God we turn from sinfulness not through fear but through love, for as our love for God increases we choose within ourselves to avoid hurting the One that we love. Sinfulness decreases as love increases.

Take what time you can to meditate on God's word as we find it in the scriptures and in so many other places in our lives. Always, always offer God your prayers of praise and thanks.

WEEK 3
Tuesday

To Win The Race

". . . and let us run with perseverance the race marked out for us. Let us fix our eyes on Jesus, . . ."
Hebrews 12:1, 2 NIV

If you would win a race My beloved, then you must strive to win.

You cannot win a race by asking everyone else to run backward so that you might be first.

No. For to win a race you must move forward. You must accomplish a goal. You must move ahead consistently and keep your eyes fixed on the point of winning.

You cannot sit and let the finish line come to you and say "there, I have touched the finish line, so I have won the race."

No. That is not your accomplishment, that is the accomplishment of the finish line coming to you.

And I am your finish line in the race to save your spirit.

And if I come to you then you have touched the finish line but you have not run your race.

No. You must see that the race is yours to run.

And though I may come to you and touch you it is only to show you the reward that is to be yours if you will run your race.

It is you who must come to Me.

It is you who must keep your eyes fixed on Me and know that you must accomplish the distance between where you stand and where I am.

Could I make this any clearer?

You are the contestant.

You are the runner.

You must stand in courage and in readiness.

I can touch you in strength, I can beckon you in love, but it is you who must bend to the task of running the race.

Not against others, but the race is against yourself.

And if your flesh is the stronger then you will sit in idleness, being deceived into thinking that there is always another day to enter the race.

But if your spirit gathers strength and direction in Me, then should your feet move swiftly and constantly to reach Me.

A race?

Yes.

A race of death or life.

Nothing has more meaning to you than this race.

Do not be lured into the crowd who stand at the sidelines with a raucous outcry.

Do not be lured into stopping in order to satisfy the flesh needs.

No. Once begun, once touched by Me to sound your start, then you must surge forth with a right and diligent heart.

Fly with a speed that is heart searching.

Run swiftly with all your might, else the flesh will overtake you and trip you in your pace.

Oh, My beloved.

I speak never a falsehood to you but I speak in the truth that is in the Spirit of God.

I speak only to guide you and to help you.

If you will hear Me then you will gain courage.

If you will hear Me then you will gain strength.

The race is to the swift and the strong. Be strong of heart then. Be strong of spirit.

And let your swiftness be in your daily praise of God.

I deceive you not. For your strength lies within and your spirit lies within.

Do not see yourself as the person in the mirror for that is a deception. You are not truly that person of the flesh, but rather you are the person who is in your heart.

And there is the race and there is the contest.

Will your heart be fixed on Me and will you run the course of My path? Or will you laden your pockets with the coins of the world and slow your progress to Me to the point where you gain the world yet lose the race of the spirit? Will you gain the world yet lose your place in My kingdom?

Beloved,
I ask you to do nothing that is not within your power to do.
I ask you to do nothing that you cannot do.
You were put in the race by My salvation. By God's grace you were brought to the starting line. And by My life and by My words you are given shoes for the race.
See Me then at the finish line.
See Me as the reward for your effort.
Beloved, fly with all speed to Me, never looking back. Look only ahead and to neither side.
There is only one purpose for you and that is to win your race. That purpose is to deliver your spirit to Me with all swiftness. Your purpose is in Jesus. And your reward is in Jesus.
Hallelujah!
Run with joy in your heart.

Through all of the teachings of Jesus He tells us that He dwells within us. Our life is within. Our spirit is within. Our race is within. Then this is where we must venture, this is where we must search. Within. There it is that we will find ourselves and there it is that we shall find God with us.

It is so very simple. Most of us try to study and to find God with our intellect, with logical thinking. But children find God through love alone. God finds children through love alone. Here is what we must do. We must cast off the cloudiness of our human intellect and search only in love. The love within. We must each search of ourselves. In quietness. In prayer. One on one with God. Some may be afraid to be one on one with God. But He truly loves us, each one. Cast fear away. And feel only love. God is love. Our spirits are love. For we are truly meant to be one with God.

In the quietness of your meditation time allow yourself to relax completely so that the flesh is stilled. Then allow your spirit to reach out. Allow your spirit to touch God, to speak to God. Listen in your spirit as God speaks to you. Here is your true communion with God. Spirit to spirit.

In closing your communion time, and throughout the day, bless God in your prayers, and offer Him your thanks for His goodness.

WEEK 3
Wednesday

In The Light

> "In him was life, and that life was the light of men. The light shines in the darkness, ..."
>
> John 1:4, 5 NIV

Keep not sorrow in your heart, but let joy be there. Sorrow is about you but you need not let it swallow you and shut you away.

No. See the sorrow but do not let it be the conqueror of you, but rather you be the conqueror of sorrow.

How do you conquer sorrow? See beyond it. For sorrow is not all-consuming. Sorrow is but the shadow that follows the cloud as it moves through the sky.

And the shadow of the cloud passes over mountain and plain. Now this house, then another house, but always moving. Never dwelling too long. Bringing a darkness for a moment but then the sun appears again and the shadow of sorrow moves on.

How do you conquer sorrow? Know that the sun shall soon fall on you again.

Do not dwell upon the darkness of the shadow but rather look out the window and see that the sunshine is approaching again. And look to the sky and see that the cloud above you is small compared to the wide beauty of the blue sky. See the immensity of the joy that is about you and the smallness of the cloud of sorrow.

Those who would rather dwell in sorrow do so by closing their eyes and cursing the darkness. Yet all they need do is to open their eyes and see the light that is close upon them.

How do you conquer sorrow? By looking within yourself to see where your heart lies — would you rather dwell in sorrow or would you rather live in joy? It is a choice that you have within you.

You cannot keep the shadow of sorrow from falling upon you, but you can look beyond the shadow to see the joy of the light that approaches. And remember the light that was upon you before the shadow entered upon you, and by this look with increasing joy to the light that approaches.

Beloved, you must dwell in your house that is subject to the moving of the shadow of sorrow, but you are not subject to that shadow. For your house is mightier than the shadow and your house gives you shelter from it. And within your house can be with you a fire of warmth as the shadow passes. That fire of warmth can be our communion. For you need not be alone as the shadow passes, but rather you can be in the joy of the hosts of heaven.

Do not close your eyes and cower in a corner but rather open your eyes and throw open the window in anticipation of the return of the light.

Blessed are those who see beyond the darkness. For the joy within them brings them comfort and hope, and joy, and love. They see the light in their heart even before their eyes can catch it.

Blessed are those who will look within themselves and beyond themselves, for they grow and make progress. They do not sit in sadness, finding a deceiving comfort in sorrow. But rather they look to the truth and see that there is light beyond the darkness. And they are patient to wait for the light to come upon them. And from within they find an inner light that keeps them in comfort as they wait. And that inner light shall sustain them and provide them with the strength of comfort.

Sorrow is not meant to overcome you, but rather you are meant to overcome sorrow.

Do this then for Me. Gather your inner strength and come out from the darkened corner. Have the courage to open your eyes to see the light that approaches. And open the window of your heart to catch the first breath of that light.

Beloved, you have within you a strength that you have not yet found. You have within you a light that you have not yet found. I can bring you that light if you will ask Me. I can bring you that strength if you will ask Me. But not of Myself, for you must first make the choice of whether to dwell in darkness or whether to dwell in light. The darkness I cannot bring to you, but the light I can bring to you.

If you will see yourself as living in the light then we should dwell together. For I am not in darkness but rather I am in the light. My light precedes the darkness and My light follows the darkness. The darkness is but a passing shadow, but My light shines unending.

I am above the darkness as the sun is above the cloud. And My light is in all directions. And darkness has but one direction. Darkness only comes when the light is blocked from entering. Do not yourself be the thing that will block the light. Do not block My light from falling upon you.

My beloved, if you hear these words then you are more in the light than in the darkness. So come, take My hand and walk with Me into the fullness of the light. And dwell there forever with Me.

Jesus always teaches us that we have a free will, that it is our choice whether to live in darkness or in light. We have the choice whether to sit and watch the race or to enter the race ourselves. It is our choice whether to keep Him outside, knocking on the door of our heart, or whether we will open that door and welcome Him to us.

Our God sometimes seems very strange. He has all the power of the universe. He created us. He has the hosts of heaven. Yet He comes to us as a servant. He has washed our feet. He teaches us. He will not invade us. He will not make us His slaves. He asks only that we will ask Him to come to us, to enter into us, to dwell within us.

I admit that I do not understand these things. But I do believe them. And in believing them I have found a greater joy than I have ever known. And the joy continues each day. Yes, I have my troubles. Yes, I have my turmoil. Those who know me can testify to that. But joy is within. It dwells within me constantly. I am happier than I have ever been. It is within. I cry tears of sadness when sadness is about me. But always joy is waiting within. Jesus is waiting within. Comfort is within.

This world is filled with the clouds of sadness and uncertainty. But the darkness need only last as long as the tears of the moment, for a wonderful world awaits within. The world of the light of Jesus. The One of love.

Reject the flesh and the cloud of the flesh. And find for yourself the joy that is Jesus within. We have the choice on where we want to be, and where we want Jesus to be. Don't worry about understanding these things. Just believe.

Keep God always with you and keep on your lips your words of praise and thanks.

WEEK 3
Thursday

Facets Of The Heart

"For God . . . made his light shine in our hearts . . ."
2 Corinthians 4:6 NIV

When you call Me, I hear you. When you look for Me you will see Me. There is no distance that separates us. I know this and you must learn it. And so, I teach it to you.

Where you are, I am. Where I am, you are. There is no distance between us.

When a mother longs for a child departed from her, is that child at a distance or does that child dwell within her heart? A mother can answer this.

When a father sends his son to walk the road of life, does the son depart as he walks the road or does he dwell yet within the father's heart? A father can answer this.

Where does a person begin? Where does a person end? Where does a person dwell?

The eyes may see a figure depart, but is that figure life or shadow? What dwells in a heart dwells forever. What dwells in a heart can never be taken. And as a father and mother share the love of a child then that child dwells in three places. And as a parent has seven sons or seven daughters so then does the parent dwell in seven hearts and yet in its own.

What person is ever alone when they are shared by others? As I was shared. As I am shared.

How can I dwell in so many places? No different than you if you can understand this lesson. For you also dwell in more than one place. And more persons dwell in you than you yourself. As you submit yourself to being less and less, then the greater you become in those within whom you dwell and in those who dwell within you.

Here then, is the true life that is a person. Not what he sees in a mirror, but rather what is in the faceted reflections of his heart.

Each friend gained, a new facet.
Each child begot, a new facet.
Each act of love toward brother, toward sister, a new facet.
Each act of love toward neighbor, a new facet.
Each prayer, each praise, a facet.
Each self-denial, a facet.
Each humbling, a facet.

And so, each who is least, each who is last, shines more brilliantly than the one who would be first. And in that faceted brilliance within, I shall dwell with you, and you with Me.

There is where to look for Me. Not at some distance, but rather captured in the rainbows that spill from sparkling light within. That is My world and it is meant to be your world also.

Join Me then in this goodness. Join Me deep within where no outside disturbances can separate us. Where growth in God's love can reach to the heavens.

You are not one, but you are many. As you accept others, you grow. As you share with others, you grow. You can never spend yourself, but rather your richness increases.

A saving love.
A joyous love.
All this abounds within you if you will see it.

What more can be said than these beautiful words of God? I cannot dwell further on this for I am too absorbed in it. I cannot presume to add to that which Jesus teaches us. After all these years of knowing God I continue to be overwhelmed by His love.

Take His words to your heart. Dwell on them. Live by them.

Let us offer our prayers of praise and thanks to God for His goodness.

WEEK 3
Friday

If You Let Me

"... God sent the Spirit of his Son into our hearts, ..."
Galatians 4:6 NIV

If you let Me, I will come to dwell within you.

If you let Me, I will be in you what you cannot be of yourself.

If you let Me, I will be in possession of you, warding off evil, and bringing you salvation.

But only if you will let Me. That is why I ask you to yield. Not in submission, but to allow Me to possess you. Allow Me to bring the grace of the Holy Spirit and the gift of life.

It is you, allowing Me.

I will not take of a person what is not offered. A parent cannot demand love of a child, but rather the child must offer it from his heart. Yes, a parent can demand that a child yield to the parent's will, but that is not love. But if the child yields of his own free will, in the giving of love, then that yielding will blend the spirits of the child and parent.

Pure giving is pure accepting
And pure accepting is pure giving.
If you let Me, I will bring peace to you.
If you let Me, I will bring joy to you.
If you let Me, I will be your loving Father.
If you will not let Me, then why not?
Does the parent not know what is best for the child?
Does an infant know what is best?
Does a child, growing strong, know the best direction?
But if a child directs himself then he serves only himself. My kingdom is not of those who are self-directed. My kingdom is of those who will yield of themselves for another. My

kingdom is of those who will take the last place, allowing another to be first. My kingdom is of those who will become less and less of themselves, yielding their space to the Spirit of Light.

And the Light shall shine from them.
My kingdom is the gathering of the Light.
Be not of yourself, but be of Me.

In these years of daily communion with God I have come to understand and accept that we must at all times diminish this flesh. We must cast off, bit by bit, this person that we are on earth. For the spirit and flesh cannot occupy the same space of a person. As you diminish the flesh you allow more space for the spirit to grow within you. This is humility, the diminishing of the flesh. It is not an outward show for others to see. But rather, it is a spiritual happening.

It is in the quietness of your private room that true humility takes place. Those about you in the world will see you as they choose to see you, but it is in the presence of God alone that you will find true humility. It is between you and He. As you diminish yourself you ask God to dwell the more within you. For who is more important to us on this earth than our own flesh? And yet God does not demand that we yield our flesh to Him. We have the choice to keep ourselves or to cast ourselves off.

Our true life is the life of the spirit. If we choose to live with God then we must direct ourselves to living in the spirit. The spirit increases as the flesh decreases.

Jesus teaches us over and over of the simplicity of our life with Him. We, then, must become as simple as a child. Find the child's love in your heart and you shall find Jesus in that love.

Is God not worthy of our praise and thanks? Let us offer these to God throughout this day.

WEEK 3
Saturday
Be Diligent

"... *be diligent that ye may be found of him in peace* ..."

2 Peter 3:14 KJV

Beloved, I labor in the task of seeking those who will be Mine. And when you first give yourself to Me you are fragile and need much care.

My labor for My children is unending as is My love. You saw My love in My final agony. And you now reap My labors.

Be at peace in your heart. Rest. Let Me be the laborer until you are strong.

A child cannot labor diligently in the field for he has not grown in strength. You are learning, and that is your path for now. Learn, then. And find strength in your learning. For in this learning My desire is fulfilled, and My desire is that you keep Me with you in the moments of your day.

The more that your heart is at peace, the more you will feel My presence. And the stronger My presence, then the more easily you will come to dwell within Me. For peace in your heart will signal the absence of the flesh and the strength of the spirit.

Do you think that any spirit within Me is in turmoil? No. When you are within Me you are safe for all time.

Find this place then. Search for it. I have spoken of it and you have found the desire for it. Others are here. And there is a place for you.

Your diligence in our communion is our bond. Continue then in diligence in our communion and in your desire to dwell within Me. That which you desire shall happen if you are diligent.

As I looked at the world, so should you look at the world. See from within. Know from within. Find strength from within.

What one of us is perfect, my friends? Not one of us. But that doesn't matter. God does not expect us to be perfect, but He does expect us to strive to be perfect. And that is why God encourages us to have diligence. For when we have diligence we will strive untiringly. This is all that God asks — that we try. And He is beside us helping us. We are not alone, but Jesus does tell us that it is our responsibility to search for the key that is in our heart. It is our responsibility to search for God. He has already found us, and in particular He has already found you, the reader, else you would not be reading the words of this book.

Diligence, constancy, love. These are the words that are in God's goodness for as we meditate our love increases. Let us always and everywhere remember to bless God through our prayers of praise and thanks.

WEEK 3
Sunday

If You Look

"And surely I am with you always..."
Matthew 28:20 NIV

Where am I in all that happens about you?
    If you look you will see Me there.
I am in the events and I am in the people that happen around you.
    If you look you will see Me there.
What is said and what is done.
    If you look you will see Me there.
Beyond yourself and beyond the others.
    If you look you will see Me there.
What common bond, what link connects you to your fellow being?
    If you look you will see Me there.
As you give of yourself and as others give of themselves — as you share.
    If you look you will see Me there.
With honesty and sincerity, with pride cast off.
    If you look you will see Me there.

Do you see Me in the steps you take?
    Can you hear My voice guiding you?
Do you trust in Me?
    Are you strengthened?
Are you comforted?
    Will you stand with conviction and authority?
Do you see Me?
    Do you know that I am about you?
Do you feel My presence?

Do you find a love direction to those that you meet? Are you looking through My eyes?

You will find all of these. For I will channel My love through you. And I reach to those that should hear My voice. The servant you are. The Master am I. See through My eyes.

Now take further steps. And see clearly in love. Yield to Me. Give way to My flow of love and a channel you shall be.

We, you and I, when we are sufficiently grown and strengthened in Jesus, will be channels of His love. We should strive diligently to see through His eyes, to hear through His ears and to love through His heart. We should strive always to be as Jesus is and to be less of who we are. Then, we shall be channels of God's love, for Jesus is God's channel of love to us.

Let us praise and thank God for giving us Jesus and all that Jesus is.

WEEK 3
Sunday Praise

The Gentle Rain

The rain falls gently
    and washes over the earth
    and cleanses it.
As Jesus comes gently
    and washes over us
    and cleanses us.

How glad i am to see this gentle rain.
How glad i am to welcome this gentle Jesus.
i envy the rain
    for i should like to
    wash over the earth
    and cleanse it.
But i cannot.
i have greater the need
    for Jesus to wash over me
    and cleanse me.
And He does.

It is the gentleness of the rain
    that catches my heart.
It is the gentleness of Jesus.
    that captures my heart.
Gentleness.
Jesus is gentleness.
He does not accuse.
He does not reprimand.
He loves.

As i would walk in this rain
    and feel refreshed

and renewed
So then is my walk with Jesus;
   i am refreshed,
   i am renewed.
My joy increases.

Thank You my God
   for this gentle rain.
Thank You my God
   for this gentle Jesus.
Send Your rain upon us.
Send Your grace upon us.
Ever increase
   our newness of life.

In days past I hated rainy days. It was a bother, a nuisance. But I see the world differently now. We need rain as much as we need sunshine. God brings all good things to us. We may have difficulty at times seeing that something is good for us. We are often times blind to God's goodness. But through the teachings of Jesus, and through the growing strength and wisdom of our spirit we begin to see, we begin to learn. We begin to see through the eyes of Jesus.

I welcome the rain as I welcome the sunshine. God is in everything, everywhere. Where He is, I want to be.

I pray that our journey is bringing to you all that Jesus is bringing to me.

Let us offer to God our words of praise and thanks.

WEEK 4

Monday	It Is Simple
Tuesday	Windows
Wednesday	What You Are Is What God Sees
Thursday	Those Who Listen Are Satisfied
Friday	I Live Today
Saturday	God's Hunger
Sunday	Channels Of Love
Sunday Praise	The One Of Love

WEEK 4
Monday

It Is Simple

"If anyone acknowledges that Jesus is the Son of God, God lives in him and he in God."
1 John 4:15 NIV

Now bring this learning together. So many words. So many lessons. Too many to remember. Too many to search through each day. But your eyes have read the words, and your heart has heard the lessons.

So much to think about. So much to do. But there is not all that much that you must think about. There is not all that much that you must do.

Bring your heart always to the single thought that God is, and that you are to dwell within Him.

So many steps to take. A long, far distant path to travel. But no, do not view it as this. For you will be confused and discouraged. But see each day, each step, each moment, as a moment with God.

See only where you are now. See only where God is now. Take this moment as the moment to be with God. And the next moment. And the next. It is simple. An easy task.

See your path as only the step that you take at this moment. Why worry about future steps? Why worry about past steps? If your heart is not right at this moment, then neither the past nor the future are of any benefit to you at this moment. It is easy. It is simple.

Be solitary in your desire to be with God. If you keep God with you moment by moment as a part of your life then the past will be in God and the future will be in God. And your heart's desire will be met.

It is simple. No difficult striving. No difficult tasks. But only bringing God to live within you and desiring of yourself to live in God. This single purpose is your existence.

It is God who will cleanse you. It is God who will make you whole. Accept Him then. Deliver yourself to Him. My words, My lessons, are meant to help you, not to heap a burden on you.

You cannot change yourself, of yourself, but you can abandon yourself, you can deliver yourself to God. That is your direction. That is your task. Is it so difficult to offer yourself over to God? That is the only thing that is truly necessary.

Relax then. Be in peace. Seek God. Pursue Him. Find Him. You need but open your heart and search within.

How very easy it is for us to be with God. But somehow it is very difficult to discover the simple. Jesus speaks of the simplicity of it over and over. But you and I in our mortal flesh find this to be a difficult task. And it always will be while we live only in the senses of the flesh.

The key is to allow our spirit to breathe a new life, to come alive in Jesus. It is the hearing of God calling us, and our finding the key to open the door of our hearts to Him. After that it is simple, or seems to be simple. Once the door is open the spirit can travel freely and commune with God at any length, at any time. Finding the key and opening the door to this communion is the difficult part. After that, love flows. Communion increases from that first visit to a daily visit, then to a moment by moment presence.

This is our journey, you and I. I found the key but not without much difficulty and wondering. It is persistence that carries us through. Diligence is the byword. And yes, we must have patience with ourselves. If we have difficulty in finding the key, it is not a crime, it is not a sin. Nor is it a weakness. Whatever is to happen is in God's plan. He will send His Spirit to help us for we can do nothing of ourselves. We can do nothing without the grace of God to assist us. But we are responsible to respond to God's call. He is ready to enter into communion with us. We must search within ourselves, gain strength within ourselves. God will know of our search. It will be His joy. And your spirit will respond to His joy. The key will be found. And the communion of love will begin. And it will last through eternity.

We have a wonderful, loving God. Know this. Bless Him always. Offer prayers of thanks and praise often.

Windows

WEEK 4
Tuesday

"Then will the eyes of the blind be opened . . ."
Isaiah 35:5 NIV

Windows, my beloved.

You are given windows to see the things that are closed to your eyes.

You are given windows of the spirit to see into that which will be. To see into that which is of the next world.

You are given windows to see the answers to that which is in your heart.

I am in your heart.

I am your windows.

And so it will be for all who welcome Me and accept Me within.

I spoke of this often when I walked the earth. And I speak of this now to those who will listen.

Did I not give windows to those who were about Me, My disciples, and those who gathered about Me? Did I not give them, and all, the open gate to the new life?

And so you have come to the place of windows. Where the veil between the two lives once prevented your seeing, now the veil parts and a window appears. A window of seeing. A window of learning.

And what brings the sight to see through this window is trust. My early words of trust and faith were for this purpose, now.

Each learning, each new grace retained, is the step to the next learning, the next grace. And so, progress is made.

Your times of anxiousness are difficult for us both. For I suffer as you do, for I am with you. Do not parents suffer with their child in the child's troubles? So also do I suffer with you.

But as the child must alone bear the trouble, so also do you. But the parent can help, if the child will allow and accept. And so also can I help if you will allow and accept.

Beloved, many good things are before you. Faith and trust bring them to you.

Therefore, keep faith and keep trust.

In almost everything about me I see windows. Especially in the scriptures. There are thousands of verses in the scriptures which provide a window to glimpse God. And so also in Christian books. Many faithful pour out their hearts in witness of the joy which God brings.

Trees are windows. Flowers are windows. Stars are windows. People are windows. Our very hearts are windows.

God is there. It is for us to search for the window by which we will see Him. And, in truth, there are many windows. Have you found a window? Have you glimpsed God for even the merest fraction of a second?

God seems to be elusive. Just around the corner. Just beyond our sight. Yet He is here. This we know. It is for us to be alert and to catch the glimpse of Him which He allows.

It almost seems that God teases us. As a parent in a game of hide and seek with children. But as the parent, God allows Himself to be found so that He can share with us in the laughter and joy of those who seek and find one another. There is much joy. And the joy increases as we find one another more and more.

Our prayer time can be a time of our telling God that we have found Him and that we will not let Him go. Once we have found Him He can never truly leave our sight again. Let us offer Him a prayer of praise and thanks for the many windows that He leaves for us to find.

WEEK 4
Wednesday
What You Are Is What God Sees

"No one can come to me unless the Father who sent me draws him, . . ."
John 6:44 NIV

No one but the Father knows who is mine and who is not. Not even I know, until God stretches forth His love to one, and that love is I. And God searches about constantly for who will be Mine. His search is in the heart, for God cannot be deceived.

So, trouble yourself not of how you appear or whose company you keep. But rather be concerned of the contents of your heart. For what you are is what God sees. And by the truthfulness of your heart, God will know you.

The one moment of truth within you is what God looks for. The moment of the true confession. The moment of caring for your neighbor more than yourself — truly caring. The one moment of seeking the last place. The one moment of searching into God.

If you would desire that you receive this living touch from God then find a quiet place, and find peace in your heart, and abandon yourself of yourself and place yourself in God's hands. Yield yourself over to Him and He shall yield you to Me. Then your true life begins. Our life together begins.

It is Jesus who came to earth to bring God's salvation to us. It is Jesus who comes to our heart to bring God's love to us. We have the new covenant with God. Jesus brought that. Our eternity is secure. And it is through Jesus that it is so.

See Jesus not only as the person who walked this earth, but see Him as a person in the Trinity of God. Jesus was with God from the beginning. And for whatever measure of spiritual time there may be, Jesus was of God to the time of His visitation with us. And for all of spiritual time, Jesus is the channel of salvation. He teaches us this. We cannot prove it. We need only to accept it.

It is Jesus who calls us. It is Jesus who shepherds us. His purpose is in God our Father and for God our Father.

Here is where the blinders of faith and trust come into play. Without these blinders we might venture down a path where we think our intelligence will provide us with an answer. How many people attempt to prove in logic that God exists or does not exist. But the answers are not in the mind, they are in the heart. Reason does not enter into the picture. It is faith, trust, love, that bring us the vision that reason cannot provide.

I believe, I trust, I have faith. I cannot explain God in the Father, Son and Holy Spirit. I do not understand. But I need not understand. I need not explain. I just simply believe. It is the key that opens the door.

My prayers of praise and thanks to God are simple prayers where I thank Him for who He is and for all the gifts that He heaps upon me. I am overwhelmed by His gifts. Please join with me and we can offer our prayers of praise and thanks together. Many voices raised as one.

WEEK 4
Thursday
Those Who Listen Are Satisfied

". . . Live as children of light . . . and find out what pleases the Lord."
Ephesians 5:8, 10 NIV

So many that are born again in Me are eager to do all that is in their power to please Me and to spread their new found joy to others.

There builds within a need to perform deeds and to convert the whole world to this new life. It is the expression of the joy of the spirit within. And this joy cannot be suppressed. It is the awakening. A new life. And a growing in God.

And the new person rushes about in eagerness to bring this joy to others and to do what in their mind is needed by God. Each new person wants to be used by God, for each one feels in debt to God. What can be offered in return for this new gift? And many search about and act on many things, hoping to please God.

But God is already pleased by their accepting of Him and by their new birth in the Spirit.

In their new growth these new children of God should be mindful that it is God's will and God's plan that must be enacted for the good of all humankind.

To be used of God is to listen to Him for His direction.

God is pleased by each and every gift, but not every gift or every action is fulfilling to God's will or to God's plan. If you are truly God's new child then you will allow God to speak and to make known to you that which He desires. Not that which you desire, but that which He desires.

By bringing yourself to God's disposal at each moment you will permit God to make known to you not only what will be pleasing to Him but also what will be fruitful to His desires.

The greatest effort is needed by a child to contain his or her joy. Have you not watched small children at play? But God does not wish to diminish the joy, nor to limit the joy, but God only wishes to channel the energy of the joy into fruitful effort in His kingdom.

Those who rush about to satisfy their desire to please God through their own actions are never satisfied. But those who listen to God's direction and to God's desires find satisfaction in even the smallest accomplishment.

This knowing of God's direction and God's desire is found by simply praying to God and listening for His response. Be still for a moment and allow God to reach you. It is a moment by moment happening.

When you pray for God's graces you expect that His gifts will be everlasting. Strength, patience, understanding. How many gifts are prayed for. And many are granted. But not all are everlasting. Most gifts are for the moment, to fulfill the need at hand.

How many good saints prayed to God constantly. They found the secret to life with God. They turned to God in all things and for all things. Not in piety and total sacrifice, but only to know God's will in each thing. For they truly desired to serve God, and how better to serve God than to ask Him of His desire.

Moment by moment — that is the secret to serving — that is the secret to satisfaction — that is the secret to knowing the true comfort of God.

Many people ask for direction, but how many listen for the answer? If you truly wish to be used of God then sit still and allow God to move you rather than moving yourself.

All of God's children are saved, make no error in judgment about that. I speak only of the need to satisfy the joy of servitude toward God's desires. It is open to all but not required of all. To those of whom it is required, this is a teaching. To those of whom it is not required, these are but words of wisdom. Not all need to labor in the vineyard for the full day, but some need only appear for the final moments of reward. That is God's plan and in God's love.

Beloved, if you will hear Me this moment, then hear Me in each moment. I am the Helper of those who desire to help. I know how to be in service to God for I have accomplished His desires. Be with Me then in each moment and I will help you to fulfill your need to serve God. And you will be satisfied.

When first I entered into daily communion with God I wanted to outdo all that had ever been done for God. My heart leaped about. And I wanted to charge full steam ahead. But for some reason my feet seemed to be made of lead. I could not move even one step. That was ten years ago. And my feet are still in the same place. But my spirit has made much progress in my journey.

The teachings of Jesus have brought me to understand that there is only one person who will save the world and that person is Jesus. It is in God's plan.

My part is to simply play the part that God chooses for me. If I am the one who waits through the entire symphony to ring but one tinkling note in the triangle at the end, so be it.

It is communion with God that is our need. God will let us know His needs. And if He asks nothing of us only that we believe in Him and commune with Him then that is what we should accept. We cannot all be earth-shaking evangelists. Some of us have to be the listeners.

But we must find this for ourselves, each one of us. In our communion times, God will teach us, He will instruct us of His desires, His needs. Perhaps our gift to Him will be simply to sit quietly with Him. Our human nature leads us to want to gain the greatest favor over all others. But our spiritual nature brings us to seek the last place, to love our enemies, to direct ourselves to God alone. When you deliver yourself to God He will direct you to where He desires you to be and to do what it is that He desires you to do.

In all things, for all reasons, we should offer God our prayers of praise and thanks. His goodness is beyond our comprehension. Bless Him always.

WEEK 4
Friday

I Live Today

> *"I have made you known to them, and will continue to make you known . . ."*
>
> John 17:26 NIV

Beloved, can you accept and believe in these words that I speak today? Do you wonder over the authority and reality of these words? I will answer these and all questions of your heart. I will, in My love, speak to all today who will listen, as I spoke to others in the past who listened.

My voice did not stop, I did not cease to be when I hung on the cross. But My voice and My teachings and My truth has continued for all who will listen.

The scriptures are not dead — they are not ended — no — but they continue. Any who look back to the past ages for answers to the heart's questions will have to live in the times of the past. Teaching is for growing. And growing is for progressing.

Did teaching cease two thousand years ago? Did learning cease two thousand years ago? No. Nothing ceased. Nothing died. But I continue on and so does God's kingdom.

How foolish to live only in the past and by only the words of the past. As God progressed mankind in the scriptures so does God progress mankind today. God's story is from the very beginning and continues yet today and will continue until God wills to establish His eternal kingdom.

Continues. Yes, God continues. And humankind continues. Let us continue together. Let us walk the same path. Let us have communion together. Do not pray to a dead God of the past, but rather, I am alive, and I live today. And so do you live today as you read these words. And so, let us be together today. Let us have communion today. Let Me teach today. Bring yourself to learn today.

This world is new every day. Yesterday is gone. Tomorrow is yet to come. But today we live. All that is, is in this day. So speak. And listen. And let us have communion.

My friends, we can all understand that God's word in the scriptures is eternal. He spoke in the Old Testament and in the New Testament. And He speaks with us today. He has never ceased to speak to us. All of His words are His teachings and we can learn much from all the places where His true words are found.

God's message is clear and it is the same over and over. He speaks to us in today's words to help us in today's world just as He spoke to others in the past to help them in their world of the past.

Nothing is new, really. Jesus continues to speak to us today as He did when He walked the earth. He is still with us. We are to learn from the sacred words of the past and we are to continue to search and learn from words, the same words, that are offered to us today.

Let us offer our prayer of praise and thanks to God for His continued presence and for all that He brings to us both past and present.

WEEK 4
Saturday

God's Hunger

"I am the bread of life. He who comes to me will never go hungry, . . ."
John 6:35 NIV

If you will read My words openly and with trust, a new truth will leap into your heart this day. I have said that "the poor you will always have with you." I did not speak these words in a manner of despondency or gloom. Nor are the poor of the world to be considered as a judgment of God or a blemish to humankind.

The poor among you are but the hungering of God for nourishment that can only be provided by Christian action, the following in My path.

As your own stomach hungers for food, so too does God's appetite seek nourishment. You can satisfy your own hunger by eating food. But God's hunger can only be satisfied by the actions of you and your brothers and sisters to feed one another, both in spiritual food and in body food.

God is good and would not cause hunger or poverty simply to show His power. If you would think this then you do not know God. God is good and does not cause harm.

In creating man, God extended Himself into yet another realm of His kingdom. And in doing so God subjected Himself to the needs of this new realm. For as I felt hunger when I lived among you, so also does God feel hunger as He lives among you.

My hunger was as yours, hunger of the flesh. But God's hunger is of the spirit. And spiritual hunger is satisfied only by the conscious effort of man's spirit to grow and increase and to nourish his fellow being.

Yes, the poor among you is God's hunger. See this and you will understand. Understand this and you will realize the mission among you.

I showed you the way to satisfy God's hunger and in doing so you will also satisfy your own hunger. For with many of you, your spirit hungers in even greater measure than does your flesh hunger.

God's hunger is real. As real as the poor among you. But each one who calls upon Me and receives Me will relieve God's hunger by the portion of that which is their self and the magnitude of their spirit.

How great then is God's hunger and how much effort is required in relieving God's hunger? Measure this by the number of your poor. Measure this by the number who do not know Me. Measure this by the number who turn from God and who starve their own spirit.

The gnawing of your own conscience is the gnawing of God's hunger. For this same reason does humankind know the gnawing of hunger. That same feeling is also God's feeling. Just as a person knows joy, so does God know joy.

Think of how you are like God. You are in His image and likeness but only in a different dimension. I came through the dimension and dwelt among you. God seeks only the time when you will come through the dimension to be with Him.

So then feed yourself and feed the poor. Pray for and seek your daily bread. But pray and seek further to nourish your spirit and your brother's and your sister's spirit.

Seek to satisfy God's hunger. His hunger is for you. Give to God His daily bread as He gives to you your daily bread.

Have we not all wept in grief when we witness the magnitude of the poor and homeless among us? How many of us are poor and homeless of spirit? We have more to look at, more to be aware of, than a hungering of the stomach. We need to see the hungering spirit that is within us and others.

It is easy to see what is before us in this world, and many turn from it either in ignorance, in shame, or in embarrassment. But God calls on us to see not only what is before us in this world, the poor and the homeless, but He calls on us to also see through His eyes the poor in spirit, the homeless in spirit. We have these with us also.

Let us offer God a prayer of praise and thanks for His truths and for the love with which He speaks to us and teaches us.

Channels Of Love

WEEK 4
Sunday

"Be devoted to one another in brotherly love."
Romans 12:10 NIV

My beloved, if you desire to love, then you should also desire to be loved. For the balance of love is in the receiving and the giving of love. The cycle of love.
I love you. You love someone else. They in turn love Me. Another cycle of love.
All the powers of God flow through love. Channels are needed. Channels of faith. Channels of love. Power flows through channels.
Then make channels. Between you and Me. Between yourself and others. Allow Me to love you. Allow yourself to love others.
If you have difficulty in loving those about you, then see Me in them and love Me in them, for surely I am there. And allow them to see Me in you so that they may also love you.
Do you see? I am the center of all love. Love Me and you will love others. Love others and you will love Me.
Keep Me within you and we shall share together the power of God's love. You and I and all others. And we are all one.

Simplicity, my friends. Does Jesus ask anything too difficult for us? He simply loves us and asks us to love others. It may seem to be a difficult thing to do but Jesus only asks that the love be in our hearts. Once the love is confirmed within, once our love is blended with Jesus' love we will then have the strength and courage to allow the love to overflow outside of ourselves.

It is all very simple. We need not make it difficult nor need we do it immediately. One thing to learn is to never lead Jesus, but rather let Him lead us. If we try to lead we will surely fail, but if we follow Jesus we are sure to keep our feet in the right path. Jesus tells us often to relax, to be ourselves. If we try to run too fast we shall fall. Jesus will set the pace for us.

Our prayers are an exchange of love with God. Exchange this love often. We should always, at all times, offer God our prayers of praise and thanks.

WEEK 4
Sunday Praise

The One Of Love

    i wake with love in my heart;
      my flesh is confused for my loved one
         is not in the sight of my eyes.
It is my spirit who is fired with love
    for within my heart dwells the
        One of Love, my God, my Lord.
It is within, that love arises
    different than ever before;
        an all-consuming love.
A full desire, a reaching out,
    a drawing in, this love
        that is like no other.
No word need be spoken;
    no motion or deed need be done.
Quietly is the bonding done;
    from within are we mingled
        and completeness binds we two.
Quiet love, gentle love, fiery love;
    a shout of joy, a silent prayer;
        my God calls me to Himself.
My spirit bursts in joy,
    yet in quietness does it
        share the lingering of love.

What is this love that calls me;
    that conquers me, that comforts me,
        that draws me to the goodness of the Good.
My heart beats loudly;
    it is real this love
        and yet so very silent within.
How can i tell anyone of this joy

>   except to those who are also
>   consumed by this same One of Love
> Then perhaps i can tell the whole world
>   for He is in this world
>   and about the entirety of it.
> And He enters in love
>   and He brings love
>   and none will ever be the same.
> Hear my words then and read my heart
>   and share with me
>   this Love Divine.
> Father, Son and Spirit,
>   over all, within all,
>   and for all.
> Yours and mine to accept
>   and welcome to ourselves;
>   this new love, this new life.

Quietly is the bonding done, the bonding of God with His chosen. It is quietness that gains God's attention and it is in quietness that our communion is deepest. Join with me in this quietness. In your private room, or your private corner, know the quietness of God's exchange, of His comfort, of His presence.

Quietly offer God, this One of Love, your prayer of praise and thanks.

WEEK 5

Monday	Your Choice
Tuesday	Purified As In A Furnace
Wednesday	A New Awakening
Thursday	Many Lessons, Many Places
Friday	Seek More Diligently
Saturday	God's Answer
Sunday	Prayers Of The Heart
Sunday Praise	Small Understandings

WEEK 5
Monday

Your Choice

"You have been a refuge for the poor, a refuge for the needy in his distress, a shelter from the storm . . ."
Isaiah 25:4 NIV

You must come to know in your heart, My beloved, that I do not cause the problems that come upon you, the storms of life, but I am in control of them if you will let Me be. I bring comfort and peace. I do not bring anguish and worry.

I have created the world and all that is in it. But through My love for you I have given you free will and a free world. I do not make you or nature My slave.

And so, though I am with you at all times, and dwell with you if you will have Me, I stand afar off to allow you freedom. If you choose the freedom to be apart from Me then so let it be. If you choose that I will dwell with you so let it be.

Apart from Me you will not feel or know My comfort. Dwelling with Me shall bring you comfort, for though the storms of nature or flesh rage about you, I am protecting you.

Being in the world you are subject to the world. But keeping Me with you will keep comfort with you, strength with you. And you will know that you are safe in any storm.

The power lies within you to make the choice of your own destiny. That is My gift to you.

And the choice of your destiny is very simply to choose to be with Me or choose to be apart from Me. From this choice all of your life will be governed.

It is not difficult or overpowering. It is very simple. Make your choice and tell Me what that choice is. And your life is governed by your choice. Rely upon yourself or rely upon Me. Be your own person living apart from Me, or be My child dwelling with Me.

There are no hidden promises or hidden threats. It is all very simple and very direct. Stand against your storms alone, or stand upon My indwelling and inner strength.

I do not control nature but I command it. I do not enslave you but I can protect you. If you would have peace with you then keep Me with you. If you would have shelter from the storm then dwell in My house.

Peace is yours for the asking. Safety is yours for the seeking. The rain may beat upon your face but I will dwell within you and you will have no fears.

Make your choice and tell Me of it.

It is to me somewhat fearsome to think that God will leave us entirely alone if we so choose. I do not want to be alone. Subject to the forces of nature. Subject to the plots of Satan. I do not want to fall into evil. I choose to follow good.

This free will is really an awesome burden. But we must recognize it and understand that God does not wish to enslave us. We are as children who leave our house upon reaching maturity. It is our choice on whether to leave forever or to return. We can live at a distance or live close.

God chooses to live close to us and to be always with us. We are free to accept Him or to reject Him. His is a true love. Can we bring ourselves to the same true love?

Offer your love to God as He offers His love to you. And offer Him also your praise and thanks.

WEEK 5
Tuesday

Purified As In A Furnace

"And the words of the Lord are flawless, like silver refined in a furnace . . ."
                                    Psalm 12:6 NIV

My beloved, you are concerned for those about you who are in turmoil, but hear these words, that when their turmoil is finished then they can come to know Me. Then they can know true happiness. They are not abandoned, those who are in torment. They are subject to the forces of evil as is the steel in the furnace. And at the proper point the finest of steel is drawn from the furnace and the slag of evil is left to harden and be cast away.

You must be purified as in a furnace. The Lord cannot accept a spirit that has not been fired and tempered to meet His needs. From that point I shall be the blacksmith and I shall fashion you into the instrument that best serves My need and the need of My Father. So when you feel strong forces, they may be the hammer blows on the anvil as you are being fashioned.

But My beloved, let it be known that even after I fashion you to meet My purposes, you are still subject to the corrosion of Satan. He will continue to act upon you and to turn you to rust. And indeed, you shall turn to rust and be of no more use to Me unless you continue to act as the instrument to which you were fashioned. Once fashioned, you must continue to plow the fields, to draw the nets, to preach My word, to hear My words, and to act upon My words.

Oh yes, Satan grows fierce as he loses souls. He musters all his forces against you. Satan hates to lose, My beloved, and he tries continually to turn you to rust.

Stay close to Me, My beloved. Let Me use you every day so that you will remain sharp and useful, and I can use you to cut into the evil of the world. We will cut Satan loose from your fellow man, one by one. Then, when I return, I will be able to reap all those who have been cut loose.

So act swiftly. All My instruments must let My hand act upon them to serve their purpose. I must work swiftly to accomplish My Father's will. Save My souls, you who labor for Me. Cut them loose as quickly as possible. Your Lord comes to reap the harvest of your labors.

While Jesus teaches us of His peace and our place with Him, He also knows and teaches us of the turmoil that is in our world. It is a part of our world as is evil a part of our world. We need His strength and His presence with us to stand firm against the forces that are about us in this world. We will be purified and strengthened. Jesus himself suffered the forces of this world. He is with us as we also are buffeted by these same forces. He provided salvation for us and truly we are saved by His loving hand. It is our believing in Him, our communion with Him, and our journeying with Him that will sustain us and bring us to His kingdom and His eternal peace.

With thanks in our hearts we can read from the scriptures and offer to our true God a prayer of praise and thanks.

WEEK 5
Wednesday

A New Awakening

> "... The hour has come for you to wake up from your slumber, because our salvation is nearer now than when we first believed."
>
> Romans 13:11 NIV

It is time for an awakening. An awakening of the spirit within which I have brought you to a new life. The time of hibernation is past. The restfulness of sleep has brought a new strength.

Awaken. Let us proceed to a new place. It is not all labor and a heavy burden. No. There is rest, and there is sleeping. And there is a new place to be.

My path bends to another place. You cannot see ahead for the place is not yet in sight. It is around the bend in the path. But if you will proceed in faith and in belief then you shall find a new joy.

The child grows and finds new words of expression. What father is not joyful to see his child grow? Do not fret the passing of time. What is to be accomplished in My Name shall be accomplished.

Your purpose now is to grow. Come to know Me. Come to trust in Me. Come to the point where you are truly Mine in trust. Then, we are one. And progress in the path is one of joy.

The steps will be easier for it is two stepping forward, not just one. Strength is multiplied. Vision is increased. Days are filled with glory. Be complete in yourself as My child. Do not be awestruck, but be open and loving. Be honest with yourself and with Me. Hide nothing from yourself or from Me. Know your full person. And disclose your full person to Me.

You have learned of David's full openness with Me. Be as this. For I would not have My child hide anything from Me. I desire full openness. The good and the bad. Then I know that you fully trust Me. Then I can be the parent who helps the child in all things.

But I must know from you all those things in which you need help. Yes, in My wisdom I know your needs. But do you have the wisdom to know your true needs, and do you share them with Me so that we can accomplish them together? There is the key to your happiness.

Share with Me and I share with you. This grows into oneness. And oneness with Me is holiness and joy and the new life fulfilled.

Rather than prayer, have discussion with Me, a time of communion. I am not the stern Father. I am the loving Father.

Honest and open discussion. That is our new place to be. Carry this with you through your day — through our day — and you will find a new joy, a new security. Troubles and anxieties will dissipate into nothingness. A new awakening.

God asks us to take a new step of faith. He asks us to disclose to Him all the secrets of our heart. He knows them already, each one, but for us to grow in Him we must learn to trust Him completely. And for us to open our hearts to Him. These sins that burden our hearts, the hurts that we have caused others, the wrongs that we have done are as a lead weight which weighs us down and prevents us from making strides in our journey.

Cast these burdens off then, these lead weights. And they are cast off quite easily, by simply disclosing them one by one to God. In my unburdening I took pencil and paper and listed each burden, each sin, each hurt, each wrongdoing. God was present as I did this. He then directed me to tear the paper and to throw it away. My sins are acknowledged and dispensed with. The communion with God that followed was filled with much love and joy. God is love and He is joy and we as His children are meant to be with Him in this love and joy. It is Jesus that brings this about.

Join with me daily, not only in our journey, but in offering God our prayers of praise and thanks for His goodness.

WEEK 5
Thursday
Many Lessons, Many Places

". . . Now, I have put my words in your mouth."
Jeremiah 1:9 NIV

The lessons you learn are many. And they are meant to be many. And they are meant to be learned. For My finger points in many places and from all these places shall you see that which I desire you to see.

For each one of you is as important as all the rest. The least or the greatest is one child and one child only.

Do not measure yourself as the world measures you, but measure yourself as I measure you.

I will take My love, My patience and My time to instruct you in My ways. Even the least of all My children is as worthy as any other. The last is first and the first is last. For I am in all things at all times.

Find more openness in your heart. Empty yourself more of self, providing more room within for Me and My love. Never lose faith and never waiver in faith, for this solidifies trust, an endless trust. Oh yes, look for My lessons in all things that are about you. My words come to you in our communion, but My finger points to other learnings throughout your day. You are wise to see and to obey and to understand.

My children are wonderful indeed, and this Father's heart is filled with joy.

The most wonderful thing that happens on your journey with Jesus is that He brings new things before you all the time. Just when you begin to think that you are at a still point, Jesus suddenly points to something new and your heart leaps and you are again in wonder. It is like that. Small insights. Sudden discoveries. That's it. Your journey with Jesus is a series of sudden discoveries. Even though something inside of you says that you knew that before, it is startlingly new because now you see it through God's eyes.

There are times when God brings us to a plateau of learning and He allows us to rest there awhile. A respite is good. And after you are rested God will suddenly take you upward to new heights of learning.

This is a wonderful journey. I hope all who are on this journey with me are continuing to learn, continuing to grow, and continuing to open your hearts to the Person who I call "Wonderful." That is who my God is, He is Wonderful.

Join me daily in our journey in praising and thanking God for His wonderfulness.

WEEK 5
Friday

Seek More Diligently

"Seek the Lord while he may be found; call on him while he is near."
Isaiah 55:6 NIV

In all that you do, keep a simple heart. Be honest and upright. Learn the one lesson to love your neighbor as yourself. In all things do unto others as you would do to Me.

For truly, that which you do to others is being done to Me. Do not reason why or how, but only know that I have said it to be.

Treat your neighbor as you would treat Me. And also do unto yourself as you would have Me do unto you. For you also are of great value to Me even as your neighbor is of great value to Me.

Listen to My words and have confidence that you have heard. Hold that which I say to be dear in your heart. I waste not one word as you should waste not one breath.

For your time in the world is very short and your time is needed for a reparation and preparation. There is purpose in your being as there is purpose in My being. And we are one in our cause to our Father.

I can but relate what you can learn. And you can learn but what is in your capacity to learn. But continued seeking shall bring continued learning. And continued learning increases the revelation that I can bring to you. There is joy in heaven for each step of learning by those who are faithful. Not one person is overlooked. Not one step is unnoticed.

Seek more diligently. Learn more completely. For complete trust brings complete joy. And God's blessedness flows to those who seek Him.

Trouble not over the daily burdens of the world, but look beyond them. For no person is a beast of burden, but each person is precious unto God. Each person is the image and spirit of God whence you came to be. Believe this and seek to know the fullness of it and you shall be relieved of the burden. And your joy will exceed all else.

Jesus brings your everyday life into very clear focus by saying "that which you do to others is being done to Me." This is a very sobering thought, especially for those of us who have considered ourselves and our actions toward others to be of little consequence. Whatever we do, you and I, to any other person, we are doing to our very God. It is no wonder that Jesus said to love your neighbor for God truly wants us to love Him. If we love our neighbor we love God. If we love God we love our neighbor. Our world shrinks to one of love.

Many times Jesus calls us to be diligent, to be persistent. Jesus honors these qualities. Our diligence and persistence is not a wearisome burden but rather it is a watchword, for if we lose diligence and persistence then we will let fall the blinders of faith and trust. We will hear the call of those who sit at the sidelines instead of joining in the race. That is why we need to be on a daily journey. One hour a week on Sunday is not enough to sustain the nourishment that our spirits require. We need the daily bread of life. We need an hourly drink of the Living Waters. We need continuing strength and diligence.

Join with me in the fellowship of diligence. Join with me in this most wonderful of journeys. God shall sustain us, you and I.

And join with me at all times also in offering our praise and thanks to God.

WEEK 5
Saturday

God's Answer

"He has made everything beautiful in its time. He has also set eternity in the hearts of men; yet they cannot fathom what God has done from beginning to end."
Ecclesiastes 3:11 NIV

Consider the words of prayer that a man "receives nothing that he asks for but everything that he hopes for."* It is good to consider this. For that which you ask for may not be to your benefit, at least in the form that you ask for it.

What I say in this lesson is that what you ask for and what you receive may be one and the same, but the form of the giving and the receiving may be different from that which is asked.

Your prayers may indeed be answered more frequently than you perceive, but the form of the answer may not be clear to you. When it seems that prayers are not answered, pay attention, for the answering may be done though you do not understand the answer.

The writer of the prayer said, "I asked for all things that I might enjoy life, I was given life that I might enjoy all things." And so the writer of that confession realized that his prayers had been answered. He asked for one thing but was given another. But that which he was given was for his purpose and God's purpose and provided more than he asked for.

God's answer is the right answer even though your request may not be the right request. See this and understand it. In an earlier lesson I had told you that a loving father would not hand a sharp knife to his child no matter how much the child would cry and beg for it. And I am the loving Father. I will not grant that which would bring you harm.

---

*Anonymous Confederate Soldier

But I will grant you growth, and strength, and wisdom, so that in maturing you might receive that knife and use it wisely in your craft. The child does not always know what is best. The Father does.

The writer also said "I asked for power that I might have the praise of men, I was given weakness that I might feel the need of God." The writer received that which he needed the most and that which blessed him.

That writer had accepted his gifts and understood in his heart that though he appeared to receive the oppcsite of that which he asked for, he did receive exactly that which he required.

The person who receives the same as that writer is blest. For the glad receiving brings joy to both the giver and the receiver.

Ponder much on the writings of that soldier fcr his spirit walked strong. And he is received into his Father's house and joy is eternal.

The form of answered prayer may not be to your understanding, but if you believe, then you trust. And if you trust then you receive. I cannot speak more plainly — it is your heart that must understand.

The writer said "I got nothing that I asked for but everything that I had hoped for." His heart understood. And so, bring your heart to understand. Look to see that you are not abandoned. Your prayers are not cast away and unanswered. The answer is there, or will be, but you must be able to discern it. And the discerning, understanding, will bring you joy. The joy that you will be, among all people, most richly blessed.

Jesus always speaks very plainly to us in these teachings. It is for us to bring our hearts to an understanding. We must study and search until we learn. It is much the same as when we first studied arithmetic in our first grade. We were told over and over that one plus one equals two. And though we learned to repeat the correct answer, it is not until we discover the reality of what one thing is plus another thing to then equal two things that we come to understand the lesson. And we cannot proceed to two plus two equals four until we understand one plus one equals two. It is for this reason that Jesus teaches us the same lesson in many different ways until we come to understand. And from that first step we are then prepared to take the next step. Learning is such a process.

But there is no need for concern. We need not feel that we have to rush forward. Jesus is the teacher. We are the pupils. Jesus charts the course. We follow. We have an eternity for learning and sharing in the joy. Let the Shepherd lead us.

Join with me please in offering our highest praise and our heartfelt thanks to our God who is so very good to us.

WEEK 5
Sunday

Prayers Of The Heart

"He will teach us his ways so that we may walk in his paths."
                                               Isaiah 2:3 NIV

You are wise and good to listen to My words. For Mine are the words of wisdom. It may trouble you that My manner of speech is not as your world's speech. But remember that I am not of your world though I did create it. And I have no need of speech other than in My teachings to you and in our communion. For humankind, though supreme on earth is yet lowly as measured by the angels. And I and My world is the realm of the angelic spirits where speech is not necessary.

But listen then to My speech and learn from it. For as God speaks, I speak. Those prayers of your heart, unspoken, but yet sent forth in love, are worth more than the silken oratory of a high priest. God's heart listens to the heart of love. Know that your message of the heart is heard.

And if you are truly wise you shall know that I send messages also of the heart for your learning. You need not hear words to know that I am in communion with you. My directions need not be in the spoken word.

But to write and read and converse words are necessary for those of the earth. But those in the spirit have communion in the spirit and words are not necessary.

As you learn then, learn this — that your heartfelt prayers are conveyed to Me. For I am with My own and I dwell within their hearts. And there is our communion.

Have heartfelt thanks. Have heartfelt praise. For truly, communion with a loved one is joy.

I speak to you for your learning. But what is meant for one is not always meant for all. For each is at a different step, and the needs of one are not always the needs of another.

Be firm in your commitment with Me. Snares and temptations await the wayward step.

Be keen of eye and wise. Each step is beyond the last and much is accomplished in your steps. Continue to study, to seek. For only in faithfulness will you be safe and grow in strength.

Keep a strong trust. Keep a strong faith. Keep with Me each moment of each day. And I am with you.

How many of us hear the wonderful words of prayer as spoken by a minister, an evangelist, a priest, a religious, and we are in awe and feel very insecure in ourselves for we lack such a talent. That is truly me. For I am somewhat tongue-tied and sporadic in my vocal utterances of prayer. But Jesus teaches us that words are of little or no value. It is what is said in the heart that counts. It takes beautiful words to fill the collection plates on Sunday, but it takes a beautiful heart to find the treasure of heaven.

Speak with Jesus as spirit to Spirit. For that is the true communion which we seek. Love is in the heart and that is where our communion with God is held. For Jesus dwells within. He has told us so. And so, we must come to believe this and try to understand it. And so we shall as we continue on in our journey.

Join me in quiet communion with God. Join me in an unspoken but heartfelt prayer of praise and thanks to our wonderful God. Hallelujah.

WEEK 5
Sunday Praise
Small Understandings

What is this wondrous gift
   that You have placed within me, Lord?
A change.
   A change within myself.
i have prayed
   for a resolution to my life
And Your way to resolve my life
   was not to change others,
      but to change me.
How wonderful;
   that which has blinded me
      has been removed.
The mistrust in my heart
   has been changed to trust.
Your strength, Lord,
   has enabled me to trust;
      to trust more in myself.
And a dark cloud has lifted;
   a burden is removed.
Yes, Lord, i have found that prayers
   are heard in Your heart
      and that You answer
      from Your heart.
Oh, so much is still
   beyond my understanding.
But i do learn;
   ever so slowly do i learn,
      for i am dimwitted.
      i am slow to learn.

i so thank You for Your lessons, Lord.
   How quickly a problem is solved

when You place Your grace
within us.
And all within Your time.
This seems to be the most difficult
lesson to learn —
that You do answer our prayers,
but in Your time,
and in the manner
that is according to Your will.
And Your manner
is for our good,
of this i am sure.
But i think that we are
mostly blind to this.
It is again, a thing
that i do not understand.

But if i was all-knowing
then i should be You, my God,
for You are the only one
who is all-knowing.
i am but an infant
filled with wonder.
But by Your mercy
my heart is light today.
A burden is lifted.
i am changed for the better,
and Your strength and patience
continue to be with me.
Thank You, Lord
for Your in-dwelling.
Thank You for Your manner
of bestowing Your grace
upon us.
Thank You for the small understandings
that come to us, for surely
to see Your full majesty

       in one moment
    would overwhelm us.
Thank You for Your lessons
    and for our slow learning;
    for we grow in small steps
       over many lessons.

It is a lifetime of
    growing in You, my God.
For as You have taught me in the past,
    our life on this earth
    is likened to a new life
       growing
    in a mother's womb.
This earth is Your womb, my God
    and upon our departing this womb
       we will be born
       into Your arms.
i understand.
And i marvel
    at Your disclosure.

Keep always with me, my Lord,
    in all things
       and at all times.
For the one thing that i seek
    is to be born
    into Your arms.

My friends, I can only suggest to you now that you form your own prayer in your own heart. Perhaps writing will help you to let the words of your heart flow. God does not need words but many times we do — it seems to be the only way to express ourselves at times. Do whatever it is that you can do.

The one thing that we should always remember to do is to offer our praise and our thanks.

WEEK 6

Monday	His Call Of Love
Tuesday	As God Would Have It
Wednesday	Travel Onward
Thursday	This Schoolroom
Friday	Stones Of Burden
Saturday	I Work Good In All Things
Sunday	My Gifts Are Yours From The Beginning
Sunday Praise	In This Stillness Of Night

WEEK 6
Monday

His Call Of Love

"But God demonstrates his own love for us . . ."
Romans 5:8 NIV

Take your lesson this morning from the woman who sat in her windowless apartment and knew that although she sat alone in a dimly lit room, that just beyond her door was a beautiful spring morning alive with sunlight and the surroundings of an awakening world.

So it is, even as you walk about in your world. For even in your world you are in a dim light and feel alone. But just beyond the door of your life is a place of eternal beauty. Of joy and singing. Of warmth and comfort.

Just beyond the door of your life is God's kingdom of eternity. And as the knowledge of the world beyond the door came to this woman's mind, so does God come to dwell with you in your life on earth that you may be aware of and learn of His kingdom which awaits you. God brings His kingdom to you and patiently awaits your commitment to dwell with Him.

Practice this for yourself — close yourself in a windowless room and think about and envision the vastness of the world that is just outside the door of your home. Then step outside and while standing there surveying the vastness of the world before you, think further of the immensity of God's kingdom that lies just beyond your world, just beyond your life.

Do you see that from a simple lesson can come a great learning?

You are never complete, you are never perfect until you enter God's kingdom. All who walk the earth need the continual lessons of God's heart. For these lessons are His call of love. Hear Him call your name. Listen to His voice as He directs you to your proper path. Through Jesus He does this. His voice. His lessons. His call of love.

I love my private room where I hold my communion with God each morning. In this private room I write these words of commitment and I slowly put together the manuscript which I hope to share with others. My private room, where I can shut out the din of the world outside.

But as I sit at my desk writing, there is a window at my left and I often gaze out upon the field and trees. There is no other house, no other person to be seen. And so while I sit alone I look out to see that there is a large world that is always there. I can watch the gentle rain falling. I can watch the birds flying about and the squirrels busily scrambling about.

Yes, there is a world beyond this private room. I am not always eager to go out into that world for it distracts me from the peacefulness that I find in my communion time. But even if I draw the shades, the world is still there. And so it is with this world. How many cling to this world, fighting to stay here, not wanting to venture on to the next. We seem to be safe here despite the turmoil and sickness. But we must travel on. We must go on into our next world. The teachings which Jesus so lovingly brings to us will help us to go on. These communion times, this journey, will bring the peacefulness, the knowledge, that God awaits us. That joy awaits us. Just beyond this room, just beyond this life.

We can know about the eternal world while we are yet in this world. Jesus brought us the good news of that. And He continues to teach us of it. There is a beautiful spring day awaiting us. There is eternal light and eternal joy. Jesus would not say it if it were not so. Your journey will bring you to know these things.

We must praise and thank God often for His beautiful heaven, for His comforting love.

WEEK 6
Tuesday

As God Would Have It

". . . I seek not mine own will, but the will of the Father which hath sent me."
John 5:30 KJV

You are concerned for the trespasses of man against man. Person against person. Of bigotry. Of hatred. Of the ills that are of the flesh against the flesh. And those ills are also against God.

Be concerned but do not be anxious of yourself. But rather come to Me. It is through Me that the changes will be brought to the world.

Do not strive on your own, but come to Me first. It is best that you first take your eyes from yourself and look upon Me.

Do not look at your fellow being harshly, but rather look upon Me with love. See Me first before you, then you will see your fellow being in the loving manner.

You have asked to see through My eyes, to love through My heart. Do this, and all your concerns, all your efforts will be right and proper.

You cannot change the world as you would have it be, nor should you look to this. But look to change the world as God would have it, and in this do not attempt to think that you know what God will want. You cannot know God's will and purpose unless He tells you of it.

Your proper station then is to come to God. Speak with Him. Tell Him of your desires. Then wait until you are moved to His will. But you may wait for a long time. And it may not happen. For your heart may not be where God's heart is.

Many desire to assist but few are chosen to assist. All who truly desire will walk in their proper path. But that path may have no requirement other than to walk in the path.

And for many this will be the cross to bear. For all who love God desire to be in His service. But He does not require service of all.

In His eyes and in His heart He will simply choose who He will. Those simply loving are in His heart in equal measure to those who labor at His tasks.

It is the desire that wins the place of honor in God's heart. Be desirous to serve. Be eager to serve. But be obedient to God's will and purpose, whether to labor or to praise, whether to toil or whether to sing. All is God's work and all is in His service.

Do you think that you do not labor when you feed the birds? That is a pleasure. But so are all God's tasks a pleasure. Learn this. For many shun their cross at the thought of suffering and labor, they think in terms of people's suffering and people's labor.

But labor in God is a pleasure. Suffering in God is a pleasure. Only those who are in God will understand.

Those who tread their own path in God's name find discomfort and obstacles. Those who tread God's path in God's name will find joy and comfort in all that they do. They do not worry about doing God's service. They have no need to be anxious over it. For they listen to God's leading and they simply follow.

That is man's greatest challenge — to dispense with himself and his own leading and to listen to God and God's leading. Man assisted Christ in carrying His cross and so also will Christ assist you, man, and woman, in carrying your cross. Do not be afraid. But trust.

We are to find God first and all else will follow. We do not perform good deeds in the hope that we will find God. But rather we are to find God first in the simplicity of our heart. Our one deed to perform is to deliver ourselves to God. Once delivered, God will point to the deeds which are His desires.

How often I sit in this private room and wish that I were a widely-traveled evangelist, bringing thousands to know of Jesus. How often I wish that I were a minister shepherding a flock of God's faithful.

At times such as that God tells me to be still and to just be with Him. He tells me that some are only to be with Him and to pray and to be in communion with Him. It doesn't seem fair to me, for some jump out into the fury of the world and fight against the odds to win souls to Christ. While here I am in the peacefulness of this room. But I choose to know God first, to deliver myself to Him. From there He will point to where I must be. My frequent prayer is, "Lord, place me where you would have me be, and to do that which you would have me do." Perhaps all that I will ever do is to sit in this private room and to hold the wonderful communion which God brings to me. If that is God's will then so shall it be.

I praise and thank God often for that which He brings to me, these beautiful teachings which bring me to know Him. Join me please in these prayers of praise and thanks.

WEEK 6
Wednesday

Travel Onward

"Your word is a lamp to my feet and a light for my path."
Psalm 119:105 NIV

To be Mine should be the desire of your heart. The young child works diligently to gain his parents' attention and his parents' recognition. The young child reaches the point of small accomplishments and seeks the approval of his parents in his accomplishments.

And so too, do those of Mine who grow as young children in the spirit seek to gain accomplishments for Me and look then for approval. It is not wrong. But it is wrong to take your eyes from Me and work toward accomplishments that are not in My Name, but rather in your own name.

It happens quickly and without notice. Much is said to be done in My Name that is not in My Name. Rather it is done in the name of the self, while loudly proclaiming that it is for Me in My Name and by My will.

Many are called to Me but not all are directed to service. Most are called to simply and justly be Mine. The returning to Me need not be an arduous journey. Nor do you need to accomplish great things in the journey. You need simply to journey.

When a person travels the road to their home it is not always, indeed it is seldom, fraught with dangers. The single most important thing is to keep your direction and be persistent in your travel. Rest at times, but do not stop. Keep your heart directed toward the end of your journey.

Who reaches the point where there is no learning yet to be gained? Is there any teacher who needs not to still be a student?

Then seek to learn more. Travel the journey of your heart. Do not stray. Do not become lost. But travel onward. With persistence. With diligence. With patience. With love.

Jesus continues in His teaching that we are to direct ourselves simply and completely to be God's child. It is not a difficult task or an arduous journey. All God asks is that we fall in love with Him. Our deeds will follow our love.

We are to become as children, simple and loving. A child trusts. A child easily loves and returns love. When I walk into one of my children's homes, a grandchild will open his or her arms wide so that I will take them and love them. That's all that God asks of us, that we see Him and that we open our arms wide to Him so that He can take us and love us.

Let us together offer praise and thanks to God for His wonderful love.

WEEK 6
Thursday

This Schoolroom

". . . we know you are a teacher who has come from God."

John 3:2 NIV

Why do you measure yourself as you do? For your measure is limited and is not lasting. People measure themselves by their wealth, by their talents, by those things that are in your world. But a person's gain in the world lasts only as long as they last in the world.

What then? Is the person gone forever and are the gains gone forever? In some it may be. But for those who find their treasure in Me then their gain is forever and they shall be forever.

For your life on earth is a searching time for your treasure. If you search the earth for treasures of the earth then you limit yourself to life on earth. But if you search your world for the treasure that is My truth then you live beyond earth and the life of man.

Your world is but a schoolroom where My children are sent to learn. And in the schoolroom who is the most important person — the teacher. And I sent you Jesus as your Teacher, and I am your Teacher.

You are My children and this schoolroom of earth is but a day in time. A short day that is filled with many activities and many teachings.

To whom do you listen? To those about you or to the Teacher? For those about you are but students also. Some more advanced, some more learned.

And you look about and measure yourself by those about you. But you should not. For your measure is but the perception that is in your heart. But rather, let the Teacher measure. You do not know the Teacher's heart, you only know your own heart. But the teaching in the schoolroom is of the Teacher's heart.

This is your learning. Take your eyes from those who are about you and look only to the Teacher. Then your concerns will vanish. Your measuring will dissipate. You will learn the true lesson that all good comes from the Teacher.

Those about you in the schoolroom are but your brothers and sisters, for you are all My children. Each one a brother. Each one a sister. Each one a neighbor in the schoolroom.

Look about to see that each one is in the same place as you. Each one is a student. Each one is a neighbor. Each one has but one Teacher before him.

Know your Teacher. And as you learn and grow then share this knowledge with others. For the one who listens to the Teacher shall learn more swiftly than the one who gazes idly at the sky and wishes for learning and for gain.

Watch the Teacher and walk the path of the Teacher if you should desire learning and gain. Join together with your brothers and sisters in your schoolroom and listen silently, but with joy and jubilation in your heart, for the heart of your Teacher is the heart of God. And from your Teacher comes the truth that is God.

From your learning of this shall come your true gain, your true treasure — and this is your life eternal with your Father.

See yourself as My child in My classroom. Place yourself in My schoolroom such that you are not distracted by others, but rather such that you can only see the Teacher. For the distractions of others will prevent you from learning, prevent you from gain, prevent your eyes from being on the Teacher.

Look straight ahead. Keep your eyes on the Teacher. There will be times of the day to share with others, to share the teaching, to share the learning, but your first effort should be to see the Teacher and listen.

From the listening shall be learning. From the learning shall be gain. From the gain shall be sharing. From the sharing shall be living. From the living shall come the life eternal. The life eternal of the Father and His children.

Know this one lesson and all other learning shall follow.

———————————

God says that we should know this lesson and all other learning shall follow. We are on a journey and the journey is in the classroom of life. And the One who precedes us is our Teacher. Jesus teaches. Jesus saves. It is that simple. We must look to ourselves and save ourselves. Jesus will tell us what to do after that. For everyone, of themselves, is to search, to find the truth, and to be born again in the spirit.

You and I are in a classroom. I am happy to be here with you and happy that you are here with me. But while we can look across the aisle and smile at each other we must remember that Jesus is before us as the Teacher and we are never to take our eyes from Him. There will be plenty of time for us to share our joy together when we are all one with Him.

And there, in eternity, can we join with the hosts of heaven in singing our never-ending song of praise and thanks.

WEEK 6
Friday

Stones Of Burden

"A time to cast away stones, and a time to gather stones together . . ."
Ecclesiastes 3:5 KJV

Beloved, I know the needs that are in your heart. I know your concerns. I know your cares. I know those things which burden you.

But speak to Me of them. For in speaking to Me of them then many will diminish in intensity.

When you carry your concerns by yourself they weigh heavily upon you. And some may seem heavier than they need be.

One stone upon another will add to a mighty burden. But call upon Me and speak to Me of each concern, each burden. And as you speak take the burden individually, as a stone, and in speaking to Me then lay each stone aside. Mark it for its concern and lay the stone, each one, aside so that we may see the total of your concerns.

With all the stones laid beside you, your burden is relieved and you can stand straight and be relieved, if only for the moment.

In that moment of relief let us commune together and share the joy of our love. Let us speak together and pray together. Let us be together in the joy and freedom that our Father offers to us.

Then together, let us look at the stones of concern and decide which ones we should pick up and act upon and which ones we should allow to lie there for us to act upon at another time. For some things are dependent upon others, or the action of others. Some things must wait until God's appointed time.

Why carry the burdens around of some future or distant happening? Be concerned only of the immediate moment.

Plan ahead, but act only on this moment's burden. Planning ahead is increasing your vision. This is good. But you should not begin to worry now about what is required later.

Praise God for the increased vision but do not labor over what you see. But carry with you today only the burdens of today. Pick up whatever stones are required for today, deal with them, dispense with them. And return tomorrow for whatever stones are there for tomorrow's action.

Always, always, keep your burden light. For you cannot travel in My path in joy if you are heavily burdened. If you must stop for a while in My path to dispense of the stones of worry, then do so. I will stop with you. For am I not here to help you?

Mine is a joyous path for it leads to our Father. But stones are heaped about, and we must have care that we are not buried beneath them. But dispense with them one at a time.

Any person can only carry one day's burden. And each day take time to unburden yourself fully and be in communion with Me. After our time together you will be refreshed and we can discern those cares which require attention today. Then let us proceed carefully, cautiously, with our eyes upon the joy that is ahead.

Is it not evident that Jesus carries the same message to us until we learn it? We are not to worry for it adds not one day to our life. But don't most of us heap these stones of worry upon our back until we are unable to move?

If we are to journey freely in this walk with Jesus then we must be free of the stones of burden. When I find myself burdened at times, Jesus instructs me to take pencil and paper and to make a list of all the things which are of concern to me. The list can be lengthy at times. But in seeing the list, I can then decide, in prayer with Jesus, which I can act upon and which I cannot. And I can do only one thing at one time.

The list frees me from worry, for in making the list I place it before Jesus for His assistance. The stones of burden are then cast aside one by one, and progress in my journey continues.

Let us together offer praise and thanks to God for His wonderful teachings.

WEEK 6
Saturday

I Work Good In All Things

"And we know that in all things God works for the good of those who love him, . . ."
                                    Romans 8:28 NIV

Beloved, be conscious of Me always. I am the God within. And for all that you do, and all the places that you go, I am with you and I am within.

I speak this in consolation to you today. For sadness is in your heart for the loss of a loved one and in your daily burden. Remember that I work good in all things. But in My workings My loved ones must keep Me with them or else My good workings will be lost.

I can and will bring good from the ill circumstances that accost you each day. But you must be aware that My help is with you.

In your free will you can turn from Me and not see the good that I bring to you. You can turn from Me to your own despair, in which place I cannot help you. In the hurt that is heaped upon you I will be with you to turn the hurt to your good. The hurt will still exist but you shall be closer to Me and a step nearer in your path.

Does the mountain climber not struggle and bruise himself in his upward climb? So shall those who trod the earth struggle and be bruised. But the reward of your struggle shall be Me. For at the end of your struggle you shall be with Me in the place of My joy. Keep this in mind as you struggle.

And as the mountain climber loses a footing and searches for a safe footing, so shall I bring the goodness of a safe footing for you in each loss of footing, each struggle, each difficulty that you encounter in your daily life.

Remember that your true life is with Me. The life you live on earth is but temporary and fleeting. Seek My life and your eternal life with Me. Allow Me, assist Me, to bring good to you from all things.

Jesus lived with us. He knows the turmoil that we face each day. Jesus is God among us. And God knows the struggles, the sadness that each of us endure. And He is with us to turn the struggle to our good. Why the world must be so I do not understand. It is God's world and I am God's child. This world will lead to God's eternity. That is all I know. That is all I need to know.

But God brings His joy in the midst of our struggles. Jesus is God's joy. He is with us now even as we struggle.

I praise you and thank you, my God, for the new life which You bring.

WEEK 6
Sunday

My Gifts Are Yours From The Beginning

"Every good and perfect gift is from above, . . ."
James 1:17 NIV

Rejoice. Rejoice My beloved. For have you not received My gift of strength and patience? That which you prayed for is now yours. But this gift has always been yours. For Mine are the receivers of all of My good graces. They are yours from the beginning but you do not realize it. You do not understand.

You have only to pray and to recognize your need. And with a right heart you become aware that you have received of the gifts that you need.

And when you pray in thanksgiving for those gifts which you have received and have not asked for, then know that these gifts are yours from the beginning but that you suddenly discover that they are about you and for your use.

Awaken then to the many gifts that are yours. Awaken and open your eyes and your heart and your mind. For I did not create you to be without Me or the gifts of My heart.

I am yours and you are Mine. And so what is Mine is yours, and what is yours is Mine. We share a common life — you and I and each one of earth. And you share in common this life with all that is around you.

Do not look so intently at the trials and disappointments that are about you. But look rather at your gifts. And rejoice. Rejoice that we are one. Rejoice that I am your God and that you know Me.

From yesterday's somber teaching we are brought alive in today's uplifting teaching of joy. "But rather look at your gifts. And rejoice."

We must be serious at times for we are in a serious place and on a serious journey. And we must at times study seriously those lessons that are placed before us. But God does not linger on seriousness, but rather He brings us to know that we are to share in His joy. We are to rejoice. We are one.

Let us in our oneness praise and thank our God who brings comfort and joy to us. In Him we are one. Bless the Lord.

WEEK 6
Sunday Praise
In This Stillness Of Night

In this time of stillness,
    this time of night,
As all about me sleep
    and my flesh is dulled in time,
My God calls
    and i arise to listen.

It is in this time of night
    that i am awakened to the quietness within;
God is constant in His calling
    and i awaken to His goodness;
The stillness is the time
    for my listening, for our quiet union.

i fly to my God
    as the moth to the light
Not knowing the full reason of flight
    but knowing that it is right.
It is dark in these hours
    yet the invisible light draws me.

i wander about
    in body and soul.
i listen and wait
    for God's joining.
i am alone
    yet dwelling with the hosts of heaven.

Here in this stillness
    is my treasure.
Here in this heart beating

is the breath of my God.
here in this hour of night
    is my being with God.

In all my nights and all my days
    shall it ever be,
For God dwells within,
    called and welcomed by His very grace.
For i am as the night sleeping
    and God awakens me to His new life.

What is Your manner Lord
    by which this is all done?
i know not,
    and i need not know.
i need but to feel Your stillness
    and know the constancy of Your love.

Wake me my God
    at Your heart's calling;
Fill me with the grace to respond
    and to lift myself in Your Presence;
Call me in this and in all hours,
    call me to Yourself.

God is always with us. More at one time than another. More in one place than another. In accordance with our needs. But it is in the stillness of night when the Holy Spirit visits us more intently. For our flesh is quiet and does not distract us.

As our flesh is dulled can our spirit fly free and mingle in oneness with God. The night can be a time of wonder, a time of freedom.

Should we not praise and thank God for the wonder of the night, for the presence of His Spirit with us.

WEEK 7

Monday	Faith
Tuesday	My Spirit
Wednesday	Many Faces, One Spirit
Thursday	Find Me First
Friday	Your Direction Is To Me
Saturday	Find Joy In Your Walk
Sunday	I Wait For Your Invitation
Sunday Praise	The Purpose Of Our Walk

WEEK 7
Monday

Faith

> "... *faith comes from hearing the message, and the message is heard through the word of Christ.*"
> *Romans 10:17 NIV*

How fragile is man in his flesh, and yet in delusion you think you are strong.

But thin and frail and fragile are you; and shallow.

Each fault pierces your skin and renders you as a sieve. A thin veil of mesh with no dimension to catch and hold the beauty of the soul. Be it though as a whisper of incense, yet the flesh cannot hold it for even a moment.

Think then upon this, and know that it is so. And think upon how you may catch the beauty of the soul. By what means, if not the flesh, can you reach and hold the beauty of the soul?

Your wealth has no value.

Your voice has no sound.

Your strength holds nothing.

And your flesh is dust.

What then have you to catch the beauty of the soul?

One thing — I have it to give, and yet I do not give it, but you must find it in Me. And that is faith. Of no measure, but beyond value. Of no depth, but boundless.

Faith.

In Me.

Your God.

In the heart of your being, in the source of your breath, in the beat of your life, it will be.

You will find it in trust, and you will catch it in love, and you will hold it in hope, and it will lead you to Me.

In your heart, on steadfast legs, is faith. The legs upon which you journey to Me. Faith brings you closer. Faith is your means, your first step. And every step to Me is through faith.

When faith stops, you stop.

When faith moves forward, you move forward.

When faith is lost, you are lost.

In your heart you know this. Find your faith. Take each step in My step.

Grow straight and true, grow full and strong, in faith. Then shall you know the beauty of the soul.

Then shall you know the beauty of God.

Then shall you know Me.

How seriously Jesus speaks of our need for faith. Faith must become a part of us as our very heartbeat is a part of us. And we find faith through trust. Then we must come to trust in our God. Through trust we will find faith and from there where faith moves forward we move forward.

Trust in God then in all things. Trust in God in each step that you take on this journey and each step then is a step of faith. The words of Jesus are here to teach us. Read the teaching again if you feel the need. For we must have trust to have faith and we must have faith for our journey.

How can we have anything but praise and thanks for this wonderful God who moves with such patience and love to bring us to Him? Let us offer our heartfelt prayer of praise and thanks to Him.

WEEK 7
Tuesday

My Spirit

". . . I will pour out my Spirit on all people."
Joel 2:28 NIV

Beloved, God has given you His Spirit. And it is called the Holy Spirit. This Spirit is the moving force of heaven and earth. Unseen to you, unknown to you, for the Holy Spirit works in the image of God, quietly and with much power. Power that would be frightening to you, and thus does He work quietly and unnoticed. This power is not frightening for it works in love.

This one almighty Spirit is the Heart of the universe and indeed beyond the universe. Come to understand this. It will bring you much peace.

Your God is not to be feared — He is to be loved. The Holy Spirit is not be turned from, but rather, He is to be welcomed. He brings life to your spirit — the nourishment of life — the power of God.

How can we praise Him enough? God has infinite wisdom and has brought it to the usefulness of all of us. You and I. God and man — but really God and spirit. For you are more than the person of flesh that you see in the mirror.

Within you is the Spirit of God — that is your true person — and that is the person that I speak to now. And it is your spirit that hears Me, not your flesh.

For it is your spirit that requires My life. It is your spirit who is My life. It is your spirit who shall be joined with Mine. Thus when I announce you to My Father it shall be as I announce Myself, for each of you who believes in Me and lives in Me is a son and daughter of God.

We are each His. Learn this. Come to know it in your heart. Believe in it and trust in it, and your days on earth will be filled with peace and your days in eternity will be filled with joy.

Bring your spirit to life. Join all spirits together with Mine and together we shall dwell in the one true Spirit, the Holy Spirit, the heart of the one true God.

In all of our journey it is the spirit within who journeys. Our bodies on the earth are but the conveyance of the spirit. Our prison, so to speak. Why it is so I do not know. But God knows.

So all of these steps are steps of faith. But our faith is founded through the power of the Holy Spirit of God. It is with us no different than those who received the Holy Spirit on Pentecost. Pentecost happens every day. The Holy Spirit moves about this earth touching those that God chooses to touch. Without that touch, that breath of life given to us, we remain in darkness. Those who desire God shall find Him but it is in God's time and through His will that the desire is consummated.

When God touches us through the Holy Spirit our spirits are set on fire. They are freed from the burden of the lost. The door is open that they may proceed to know God. The spirit comes alive as does a flame burst forth from a spark.

The Holy Spirit works very quietly. Nearly unnoticed. We, therefore, must be very attentive if we are to discover His workings.

It is by the Holy Spirit that the scriptures were written. It is by the Holy Spirit that we acquire the graces of God by which we will know Him. Give praise and thanks to God for His Spirit and the graces which abound about us.

WEEK 7
Wednesday

Many Faces, One Spirit

". . . For I tell you that their angels in heaven always see the face of my Father in heaven."
Matthew 18:10 NIV

Beloved, look in a mirror and each shall see a different face. For each person is different one from another.

But from within each person is the same. Each person's spirit is of the Spirit of God. It is the breath of life to you.

Each spirit is the same and so each person, before God, is the same.

In the mirror of the spirit each one looks the same for each one is the same. The same as Me — the same as the Father.

From one life, the life of God, springs all life. But yet, even being the same, the finger of God gives to each spirit the quality of an individual angel.

Thus, you are your person, both on earth and in heaven. You will not stand before God faceless. But God will recognize you for the person that you are.

And I shall announce you to Him for the person that you are. And the hosts of heaven will know you, and your loved ones will know you, and in the kinship of the Spirit all will know you.

My world is a marvelous world, not through My hand but by My Father's hand. But it is Mine to govern. Mine to rule. Mine to invite you in. Mine to give you peace and rest within.

How good is My kingdom yet how difficult it is for you to understand. As you progress in My path you will come to understand more, but still it will be hidden from you and you must trust.

Some who read these words do trust and their path is easier for it. Some do not trust and have much more work to do.

But each of you has the same spirit. Each of you has the same capacity to know Me. Each has the same capacity to share. Each has the same capacity to love.

Continue on in your progress. Continue on in Me.

Each one of us has the same capacity to know God. There is not one of us, in God's eyes, who is better than the rest. We are different, that is certain. There are no two people who are exactly the same. And here Jesus tells us that no two spirits, no two angels are the same. Yet God loves us equally.

Each one of us then, must come to know within that we have equal value before God. So many of us feel unworthy. But not one of us is unworthy. To show this, Jesus sat with sinners and prostitutes. He saw each person as the same. He worked with each one differently, according to each one's needs.

He does the same with us. He loves us all equally, but He works with each one differently. You are a very special and very individual person to God. Think about this for a while. It's very important. You should not allow the world to pass you by as it journeys forward. But each one of us, you, are asked to take the hand of Jesus and walk with Him. You are special. I am special. Your neighbor is special. Is that not a witness that our God is special?

Search the scriptures to see how God had dealt with people through the ages. None is different than you or I. Be open to God as He seeks you out. Praise and thank God in your prayers.

WEEK 7
Thursday

Find Me First

"For it is by grace you have been saved . . . not by works, so that no one can boast."
Ephesians 2:8, 9 NIV

Beloved, be very careful to eliminate boastfulness from your person. For this is foreign to God. Those who perform good deeds and boast of them have gained nothing for themselves. For some seek to gain heaven by man's ways and that is impossible.

You cannot buy your way into heaven with either money or good deeds. No. Any good deeds must come from your heart and be kept in secret. Others may know of them and be impressed, but that is acknowledgement on their part.

To seek praise for yourself for any good actions is against the nature of the spirit. Those who are Mine will know this. Those who are not Mine will not know this and so they desire to be in the grace of God by performing good deeds so that He will notice. But that is not the price to gain the favor of your God. The price is only that you love Him. Give Him your faith and your trust. Give Him truth and honesty.

When you come to these acts of faith then you will know Him. From that point, any good deeds that you perform shall be brought by the Holy Spirit and they shall be magnified and shall be directed in God's purpose.

First, be humble, then you shall be great. You cannot ever reach God through the ways of man. Nor can you perform service to Him without His blessing. For man is nothing unto himself until the Holy Spirit shall come upon him.

So it was with one of My most fervent servants, Paul. For Paul was nothing when he was Saul of Tarsus. Your world would not know of him in these times. Many thousands of people lived in his time, yet few are remembered. But by the grace of God, the Holy Spirit came upon Him and he performed a wondrous service to God. By the Holy Spirit only. Not by Paul. And he knew this and so you should know it.

Do not lead your Lord or attempt to win Him by good deeds done in selfishness. Spend your energies first in finding your Lord. Then there shall be time for good deeds, performed in the fervor and in the direction of God. Nothing is more important to you than to seek your Lord and to be born again in Him. Thence all other things may follow.

Worry not about your possessions for they will not be a part of My kingdom. Worry not about the poor for God knows their need. Worry about one thing — the salvation of your soul. Find this as soon as possible. Once that is gained then you shall indeed work for the poor and for the lost. See these things in God's eyes, not in man's eyes.

Work for the kingdom of God according to God's needs, not according to your needs. Let Me guide you. Let Me direct you. For many of you are as Paul was — untrusting and misguided. And so it was necessary that God direct him in the proper path. And so God blinded him that he might see properly. For too many see only the flesh and are blind to the Spirit.

But you must be directed so that you are born again in the spirit so that you can see the things of God. And you shall also see clearly the things of evil.

Your blindness must be removed. And this will be done in the Name of your Lord Jesus Christ. With that shall come the blessings of the Holy Spirit and your life in the kingdom of God.

Be directed then by God, and not by your flesh. Come to Me first before you turn your direction to the world. And permit Me to choose your purpose in life.

Seek not your own desires, but seek God's. And if you will be patient you shall come to know God's desires. But allow yourself to grow in your Lord and to know the joy of His Presence. Learn first to rejoice in your Lord, for that shall support you in your burdens. And trust, and have faith, for these shall mark My path and by these you shall follow.

Be of a humble heart. Never boast. For you are nothing in yourself but only in your God.

Find Me first and find peace.
Find Me first and find love.
Find Me first and find the Holy Spirit.
Find Me first and find your purpose.

This is a difficult lesson for most of us to learn. For it seems that we are taught as children to do good deeds. And so we should. We should always do unto others as we would have them do unto us. This is very necessary for us to live together peacefully in this world. But these good deeds are for ourselves and for our betterment alone. We do not win God's favor through these good deeds. Nor do we find God in these good deeds.

We find God in love. Our most necessary deed is to deliver ourselves to God. If we do nothing else on this earth we must search for God and deliver ourselves to Him. After that, all that we do will be in the Name of God. Opportunities for good deeds shall then be all about us. But most of them will be quiet deeds, unnoticed by others. As Jesus works with us, quietly and individually, so shall we work with others.

Our human nature wants us to stand on a street corner and loudly proclaim our good works. Our human nature feeds on boastfulness. But God abhors boastfulness, and so should we.

Direct yourself always to finding God and knowing His will in everything that you do. Allow God to direct you.

Praise and thank God always for His wonderful teachings and for His ever-present love.

WEEK 7
Friday

Your Direction Is To Me

"Trust in the Lord with all your heart and lean not on your own understanding; in all your ways acknowledge him, and he will make your paths straight."
Proverbs 3:5 & 6 NIV

Beloved, some lessons may be difficult, but they are meant to keep your direction in Me. Look to Me for guidance. Look to Me in trust.

If all of your pursuits are not in Me then many steps you take will not be favorable and will misdirect your course.

Trust that I will place your feet in each of the right steps for you.

What you might consider to be good for you may not be good for you. I will know this and I will keep you in the right steps.

Be diligent. Persevere. But do not be disappointed at losses and failures. Some of what you consider to be losses and failures in your eyes may not be so in My eyes.

Your beginning and end are in Me. Keep that ever present. And remember that your direction is not to yourself and to meet your needs, but rather your direction is to Me and to meet My needs.

The sparkle of gold should not blind your eyes, for that would lead you astray.

It will be difficult for you to sacrifice your desires for Mine, but Mine will bring you to Me.

So accept and learn. Take losses and disappointments as lessons. Learn from them. And what you learn will direct you to Me more and more.

Remember that it is My life and My kingdom that is your life and kingdom. Do not direct your own life and build your own kingdom. But come, and be with Me.

An old lesson, a new lesson. Jesus here speaks a lesson for us today that was spoken clearly in the verses of Proverbs. It is no odd coincidence that the scripture verses which lead the lesson are the same content as the lesson. God never changes, but our world changes constantly. For this reason Jesus speaks with us today, teaches us today, and journeys with us today. He is the same Jesus who is with God from the beginning. God's messages to us continue through the ages.

Read today's lessons as God speaks them today. Read the scriptures as God spoke them thousands of years ago. The message is the same. God is the same.

Read the scriptures often. Meditate upon all of God's words to us. Offer God your unending prayers of praise and thanks.

WEEK 7
Saturday

Find Joy In Your Walk

". . . no one can enter the kingdom of God unless he is born of water and the Spirit. Flesh gives birth to flesh, but the Spirit gives birth to spirit."
John 3:5 & 6 NIV

As you walk in My path do not be concerned if you find yourself alone. Do not be concerned that if you look about in your vision that you see no one — that you see a vastness that is empty of others and of other things. For to see others and other things may distract you. It is better for you to be alone with only My presence before you.

And do not be concerned that you do not see Me in the form that is familiar to your mind. But rather accept the belief of My presence.

For I am in the Spirit of God. Thus it is that your spirit accepts and welcomes My presence. For into My Spirit your spirit can join and become one with Me.

It is your flesh senses that cause you to wonder and to look about. But push this concern aside for it is not your flesh that will join with Me.

Walk, and find joy in your walk. Look only forward, and look with your eyes of the spirit.

You will grow. And you will find comfort. And you will find strength.

Keep in one direction. Keep in one purpose. The direction toward Me. The purpose to join in God's presence.

Sons and daughters, there is no greater gift than to receive the Spirit of God. There is no greater purpose than to join as one with your God. Do this, and receive the blessing and the life of God.

There are times in our journey that we may feel very much alone. But we are never alone. Jesus is always with us. We are "alone" with Him. Perhaps this frightens some of us. To be alone with God may be an awesome thought but if the Holy Spirit has awakened your spirit then the thought of being alone with God is a joyful one.

God tells us often to rejoice. And so we should. To be with God, whether alone or in the company of a fellowship is a wondrous thing.

Stay close to Jesus. Be with Him each day. Never turn from your journey.

Join in the song of those who journey with Jesus. The song of praise and thanks to God.

WEEK 7
Sunday

I Wait For Your Invitation

"I have made you known to them, and will continue to make you known in order that the love you have for me may be in them and that I myself may be in them."
John 17:26 NIV

Beloved, have you read with your heart these words which I have spoken to you? Have they merely brought a feeling of comfort to you or have you come to know your God more profitably?

Unless you render thought and action to My words they will be wasted. For man has in him a compunction of heart but he does not abide by it.

The sense of right and wrong. The small whisperings of your conscience were placed within you for your benefit. But the mad shakings of the world overpower these whisperings and so they are lost. Let it not be so with these words.

People have grown accustomed to obeying only their senses that are tuned to the world. The whirling of lights, the deafening noises, the perfumes, the fine clothes. And they look continually to increase these to the point where they have no enjoyment of the nature of the world and must magnify the more their artificial pleasures.

And this work of evil overshadows the whisperings of conscience. For when their conscience calls, many simply turn louder the music or turn to a distracting form of entertainment.

But the voice of conscience persists because it is the hand of God that placed it within. God knew that people would continually look to Him for answers and so God provided a sense of right and wrong.

Allow this voice of your angel to reach your heart. Listen and follow.

The simplicity of knowing the will of God is to turn to no one but yourself. All answers are within you.

If some appear more wise in the knowledge of God it is only that they have searched for Him earlier and found Him. But your own capacity for knowledge of God is as great as anyone else's. But you must exercise it. You must turn within yourself.

Begin your search within yourself, and begin it now. Your search, no matter where it begins must eventually lead to within yourself.

Listen to what comes from within for your voice of right and wrong is a place to begin. Allow it to speak freely and listen freely. Do not attempt to steer the voice but instead let it guide you.

You will begin to follow the proper path, and if you desire it, this path will lead to Me. For I stand and wait for your invitation. For you to invite me into your life. I created your life but I will not intrude into it. I wait to be invited. For that will be your show of love to Me. And that will make us complete.

I seek to return you to the presence of God. Listen to the whispering voice within for your spirit desires to be on the journey to God's presence.

Begin this search within yourself. And let that search deepen to a search of communion with your Lord.

Be sincere. Be truthful. Invite Me into your heart and I shall be there. And at that moment you shall also be in My heart.

Beloved, I speak to you now in words that you can read, but My voice has echoed in many ways to you.

Hear my voice and believe in it. Hear My voice and tend to it.

Do these things with love in your heart and you shall find the joy which I have promised.

The simplicity of this lesson is that God is always with you. He has placed the quiet voice of conscience in all of us from our beginning. Perhaps we lose appreciation for our conscience because it has always been there.

This lesson brings to light the necessity of the voice of conscience and if we trust in it we cannot go wrong.

Our search can begin and be strengthened by turning within. By trusting in our conscience, by listening to God's guidance, by seeking His word in scriptures, in Christian readings, and hearing His word within us.

God wants to be invited into your life. He has invited you into His life and now awaits an invitation into your life.

Spend time in contemplation of this lesson. Listen for the voice within you. Bring your conscience to be a real part of you — it is not something to be ignored or ashamed of. Your conscience is you. If you have no conscience then there is no you. If your conscience is forthright then your journey shall be clear and joyful.

Quietly and sincerely invite Jesus into your life. Offer God a joyful praise and heartfelt thanks.

Conclude with God's word in the scriptures and reviewing all that has been brought to you in His lessons.

WEEK 7
Sunday Praise
The Purpose Of Our Walk

i wait upon You in all things, my Lord.
i go about my daily tasks
    with the ear of my heart
        listening always for Your voice.
It seems at times
    that i am moving about
        in a dream
    for i am more with You in spirit
        than i am at my place of work.
You have surely captured my heart,
    my spirit, and the very person
        which was created for You.
And all of that person
    is at peace with You, Lord;
a more beautiful peace
    i have never known.
And my longing
    to be with You completely
        increases with each day.

i am but a shadow
    in this place on earth;
        i am but fragments
            of who i once was.
And i am glad,
    and i am heartened,
        for i seek to cast off
            this flesh about me,
            and to deliver myself
                totally and completely to You.
Was this not the purpose
    for which I was born?

You have been a most patient teacher, Lord,
    and i a most slow learner.
But in Your dedication,
    and through the grace of persistence
    i am gaining within
        that which You direct me to know.
i cannot claim to understand
    for i do not.
But i do know.
i am aware of Your truths, Lord,
    though Your truths seem at times
    to be wisps of light
        gliding about me,
        intangible and fleeting.
Yes, these are the glimpses of truth
    which You promised in the past.
Glimpses of truth, yes.
And this is for the best,
    for to suddenly know You
    in Your completeness
        would be overwhelming.

And so,
    i reach for the wisps of truth
        which glide about
    and i learn bit by bit, slowly,
        of Your Person,
        and Your teaching.
Ever increasing is my learning.
Ever increasing is my love.
Ever increasing is our life together,
    You within me
        and i within You.

When shall we be one?
    My heart begs to know.
Yet i need not an answer,
    for somehow
    i already know the answer

> but i have not yet fully realized it.

And is this not true
> of all Your truths, Lord?

The answers are known,
> all of the answers are within us,
> but we have not yet come to realize
> > the answers.

Is this not the purpose
> of our walk with You,
> > our journey in Your path?

Each step
> is a realization
> > of a truth.

Each truth gained
> is an increase
> > of faith.

Each increase of faith
> is a further deliverance
> of ourselves
> > to You.

Blessed are You, Lord,
> and blessed are Your ways.

Teach me Your ways, Lord.
Fill me
> with Your truths.

God be with you today and through all of your days. I pray that you have come to know His joy moment by moment in your lives.

I praise and thank you my God for your goodness and for your unending love. Thank you for this wonderful journey. Hallelujah.

"So then, just as you received Christ Jesus as Lord, continue to live in him, rooted and built up in him, strengthened in the faith as you were taught, and overflowing with thankfulness."
Colossians 2:6, 7 NIV

Please send me _____ copies of INVITATION TO A JOURNEY (Book # 7940) Enclosed please find $8.95 per copy plus tax, postage and handling.

ORDER BLANK

Qty.	Item #	Price

N.Y. state residents add 8% sales tax _____

subtotal _____

shipping & handling _____

TOTAL _____

Name _____

Address _____

City, State, Zip _____

A. When ordering from the author, please send check or money order to:

> Robert Styczynski
> PO Box 42
> Latham, NY 12110

Please add proper shipping and handling as in box below:

> 1-3 copies add $1.80
> 4-7 copies add $1.95
> 8-11 copies add $2.10
> 12 and over add $2.30

B. Or you may order from:

> Fairway Press
> 628 S. Main Street
> Lima, Ohio 45804

TAX, POSTAGE, AND HANDLING. For shipping and handling: Add $3.50 on all orders up to $20.00. On orders from $20.01 to $50.00 add $4.35. On orders over $50.00 we will add actual postage. Ohio residents add 6½% sales tax. Ohio churches and other Ohio tax exempt organizations must send us a copy of their tax certificate number.

☐ check or money order enclosed
☐ charge to my VISA
☐ charge to my MASTERCARD

card number _____ exp. date _____ signature _____